Key West

(Third Edition)

by

Sarah Goodwin-Nguyen

Key West, 3rd Edition (*Tourist Town Guides*®)
© 2011 by Sarah Goodwin-Nguyen
Published by: Channel Lake, Inc., P.O. Box 1771, New York, NY 10156-1771
http://www.touristtown.com

Author: Sarah Goodwin-Nguyen
Copyeditors: Dirk Vanderwilt, Elisa Lee
Cover Design: Julianna Lee
Maps: Eureka Cartography
Page Layout Design: Mark Mullin
Publisher: Dirk Vanderwilt

Front Cover Photos:
"Rooster at Hemingway's House" © iStockphoto.com/lroberg
"Walkway to the Beach" © Sarah Goodwin-Nguyen
"Palm Tree" © iStockphoto.com/joxxxxjo
Back Cover Photo:
"Salt Ponds" © Sarah Goodwin-Nguyen

Published in April 2011

ISBN-13: 978-1-935455-14-1

Disclaimer: The information in this book has been checked for accuracy. However, neither the publisher nor the author may be held liable for errors or omissions. *Use this book at your own risk.* To obtain the latest information, we recommend that you contact the vendors directly. If you do find an error, let us know at corrections@channellake.com

Channel Lake, Inc. is not affiliated with the vendors mentioned in this book, and the vendors have not authorized, approved or endorsed the information contained herein. This book contains the opinions of the author, and your experience may vary.

Help Our Environment!

Even when on vacation, your responsibility to protect the environment does not end. Here are some ways you can help our planet without spoiling your fun:

★ Ask your hotel staff not to clean your towels and bed linens each day. This reduces water waste and detergent pollution.

★ Turn off the lights, heater, and/or air conditioner when you leave your hotel room.

★ Use public transportation when available. Tourist trolleys are very popular, and they are usually less expensive and easier than a car.

★ Recycle everything you can, and properly dispose of rubbish in labeled receptacles.

Tourist towns consume a lot of energy. Have fun, but don't be wasteful. Please do your part to ensure that these attractions are around for future generations to visit and enjoy.

Dedicated to the wild creatures and wild people of Key West who make my every day here an adventure.

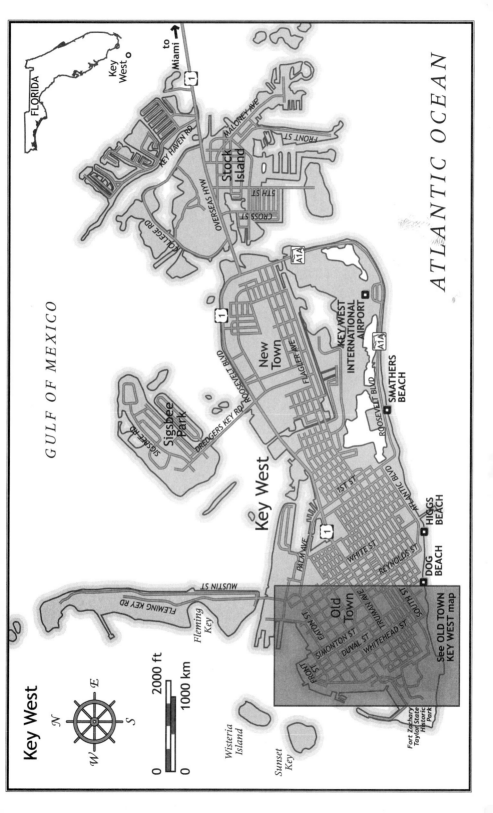

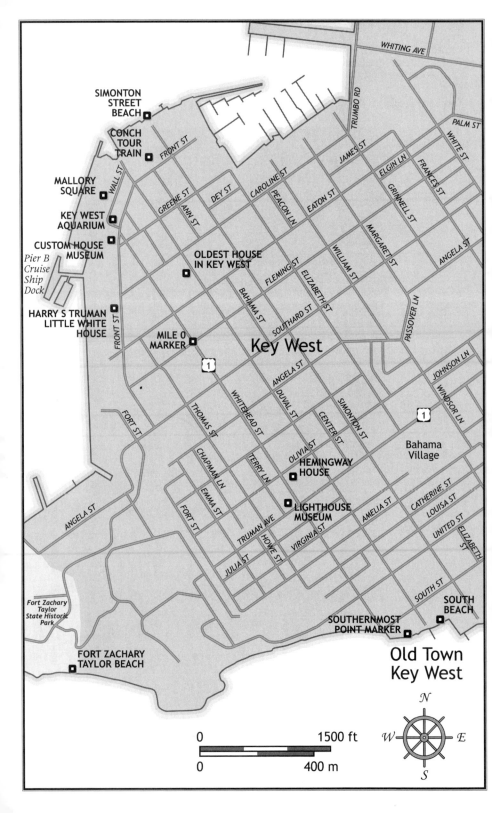

Table of Contents

How to Use this Book

Tourist Town Guides® makes it easy to find exactly what you are looking for! Just flip to a chapter or section that interests you. The tabs on the margins will help you find your way quickly.

Attractions are usually listed by subject groups. Attractions may have an address, Web site (🖱), and/or telephone number (☎) listed.

Must-See Attractions: Headlining must-see attractions, or those that are otherwise iconic or defining, are designated with the ★ Must See! symbol.

Coverage: This book is not all-inclusive. It is comprehensive, with many different options for entertainment, dining, shopping, etc. but there are many establishments not listed here.

Prices: At the end of many attraction listings is a general pricing reference, indicated by dollar signs, relative to other attractions in the region. The scale is from "$" (least expensive) to "$$$" (most expensive). Contact the attraction directly for specific pricing information.

In 1821, American businessman John Simonton purchased Key West for $2,000 from Juan Pablo Salas.

Introduction

Welcome to Key West—the last tiny island in a string of tiny islands off the coast of Florida. Geographically, Key West is closer to Cuba than to Miami. It boasts a subtropical climate with year-round temperature in the mid-seventies, so there's little need for more in your wardrobe than tee shirts and sandals. Sometimes referred to as the "American Caribbean," and sometimes, more disparagingly, the "Redneck Riviera," Key West is like no other place in the United States.

The very name "Key West" evokes iconic palm trees, tropical blue waters, ice-cold margaritas, and a laid-back island lifestyle. The island has a fascinating mixture of American, Bahamian, and Cuban cultures, all existing within one of nature's most fragile and beautiful ecosystems. With the Atlantic Ocean on one side and the Gulf of Mexico on the other, the island is protected from rough waters by the only coral reef in North America. The air is salty and floral, and the sunsets are spectacular.

Key West has charmed many a vacationer into becoming a "local". An eclectic collection of big personalities have called the island home, including Ernest Hemingway, Harry S. Truman, and Jimmy Buffett.

Key West is famous as fishing town, a drinking town, a pirates' hideaway, and an artists' retreat. There is something here for everyone—a colorful history, a vibrant arts and dining scene, hot clubs and bars, beaches and boats, fascinating marine creatures, and a wealth of wildlife.

KEY WEST HISTORY

The first recorded mention of the Florida Keys was in 1513. Spanish explorer Ponce de León, while searching for the Fountain of Youth, passed them by and made note. Crewmember Antonio de Herrera chronicled the event in his journals, writing:

> *"To all this line of islands and rock islets they gave the name of Los Martires (The Martyrs) because, seen from a distance, the rocks as they rose to view appeared like men who were suffering; and the name remained fitting because of the many that have been lost there since."*

The writing refers to ships of conquistadors capitalizing on the Gulf Stream to carry them swiftly back to Europe with their plunder, who often crashed on the reef.

When the Spanish finally came aground, they found the shore strewn with bleached bones believed to be remnants of a vicious battle between the island's tribe of Calusas versus Seminoles from the mainland. The settlers called the place "El Cayo Hueso"—"Key of Bones." The name "Key West" is believed to be an Anglicization of this more ominous original name.

The island's natives were quickly enslaved, displaced by Spanish settlers, or done-in by Western diseases. Spain controlled the Keys, including Key West, until 1763, when they traded Florida to the British in return for the port of Havana. Twenty years later, Britain gave the Keys back to Spain in an attempt to keep the islands out of the hands of the rising United States.

THE KEYS ARE BOUGHT AND SOLD

Nonetheless, after the end of the Revolutionary War, it all became American territory. In 1821, American businessman John Simonton purchased Key West for $2,000 from Juan Pablo Salas, who had acquired it as a Spanish Land Grant in 1815. Simonton divided the island into four sections, selling three of them to other businessmen: John Whitehead, John Fleming, and Pardon Greene (all four men have streets named after them Downtown). Unfortunately, Salas had also sold Key West to a lawyer named John Strong. Strong then sold Key West to General John Geddes—but also George Murray. It was all becoming a bit of a mess. However, Congress was called in to clear it up, and Simonton (who had influential friends) was declared the island's rightful owner.

Key West began its modern life as the poor victim of a land scam. But, in many ways, the Keys have always been a lawless place. Ever since the days of the Conquistadors, the Keys were plundered by Cubans for fish and sea turtles, by Bahamians for mahogany, hardwoods, and salvage of crashed ships, and by pirates who preyed upon them all (like the infamous Black Caesar, who lurked in Keys waters in the early 1700s).

PIRATES AND A MILITARY PRESENCE

John Simonton finally called upon the U.S. Navy put an end to piracy in nearby waters. Captain David Porter arrived to set up a naval base in Key West. Unfortunately, in the process, he declared martial law in Key West—and himself as military dictator. He was eventually courtmartialed after leading an invasion on Fajardo, Puerto Rico (to avenge the jailing of an officer from his fleet). But the navy has been a huge presence in Key West ever since—while the people in pirate garb that visitors see generally are dressed up for Fantasy Fest; a kind of modern-day homage to the region's colorful past.

There was often a fine line between pirates and "wreckers" who salvaged ships and their holdings that had crashed on the reef. Occasionally, ships were lured to their demise by purposefully placed markers or lanterns. In 1925, the Federal Wrecking Act barred foreigners from taking salvage from the Keys. So English Bahamians, who made up the largest part of the wrecking industry, moved en masse to the Keys, often dismantling their houses and transporting them whole. Many of these architectural delights are still standing in Key West, especially in "Bahama Village," where many of the ancestors of these original immigrants still reside.

INDUSTRY AND TRADE

The influence of the Bahamas is obvious in Key West's cuisine as well. Conch (pronounced "conk"), are large mollusk once prolific in Keys' waters, but overfishing led to its near-demise. Conch was a staple of the Bahamian diet, and, though currently protected in local waters, it is still a popular item on local menus. These days, the word "conch" has even come to refer to a person born and raised in Key West.

Fishing, hunting sea turtles, and salt manufacturing were other big Key West industries. Between 1828 and the 1850s, Key West was the richest city per capita in the United States. It was not unusual to find homes filled with lavish (if slightly water-stained) furniture, dishware, and even clothing salvaged from wrecks. By the 1850's, reef lighthouses were built, putting an end to the wrecking business.

Sponging was another popular trade in the Keys, until stocks began to dwindle. By the 1940s, overfishing and a blight had wiped out ninety percent of the Keys' sponge population. After massive efforts at restoration, sponges have made a comeback, helped largely by the invention of the synthetic sponge.

During and after the Cuban Revolution, the cigar trade traveled from nearby Cuba to Key West, employing approximately 10,000 Cubans. Cigars remained big business until tax-free land and cheaper labor enticed the factories to relocate to Tampa. The Cuban influence still looms large in Key West's cuisine, art, and music.

During the American Civil War, Florida seceded from the Union with the South in 1861. Yet Captain John Brannon and his Union soldiers manned Fort Zachary Taylor, which had recently been built to defend Key West Harbor. Fort Zach became headquarters for the U.S. Navy's Gulf Coast blockade squadron, deterring numerous supply ships from reaching Confederate ports in the Gulf of Mexico. Later, Key West would also played a pivotal role in the Spanish-American war, which liberated Cuba and the Philippines.

A BOOM IN TOURISM

In 1912, after 7 years and 20 million dollars, oil tycoon Henry Flagler completed the Florida East Coast Railway; an engineering marvel (parts of it are still standing today) running over open ocean, from Miami to Key West, for an incredible 156 miles. The age of tourism in the Keys was underway, and the town boomed with tourist dollars.

Prohibition was taken with a grain of salt in Key West, and some citizens made their fortunes bootlegging, rum running, and establishing speakeasies. Bordellos sprang up to service the sailors—as did several gay men's clubs. Capt' Tony's Saloon on Greene Street claims to be the oldest bar in town, as well as the site of the original Sloppy Joe's. Its license was issued at the repeal of Prohibition in 1933.

Unfortunately, not even Key West was immune to the Great Depression. Tourism slowed with the threat of World War II. By 1934, eighty percent of Key West's residents relied on government assistance, and Monroe County declared bankruptcy. To top it off, Flagler's railroad was destroyed during a Category 5 hurricane on Labor Day, 1935. Instead of rebuilding the railroad, the Overseas Highway would be constructed in 1938.

After World War II, Key West became known as a haven for writers. During this time, Poet Wallace Stevens brawled with Ernest Hemingway at Sloppy Joe's. Tennessee Williams and Truman Capote flirted with sailors. Elizabeth Bishop wrote many poems here, and Robert Frost wintered on the island for his health.

In 1949, a fisherman named John Salvador found many more shrimp than normal in his catch, prompting him to put the nets back overboard. This second trawl was also filled with shrimp, and "pink gold" was officially discovered. Over 300 boats quickly came to Key West, and the first full season, 1950-1951, harvested 15 million pounds of the stuff. Stone crabs, spiny lobsters, and grouper have also provided livelihoods for many commercial fishermen.

THE CONCH REPUBLIC

The groovy 1960s and 70s created yet another moneymaker for enterprising Key Westers: smuggling marijuana from Cuba. This was indirectly responsible for one of the most absurd episodes in Key West history. In 1982, the United States Border Patrol decided to set up a checkpoint at the Last Chance Saloon in Florida City. They were looking for people trafficking drugs and/or illegal refugees from Cuba through the Florida Keys. A seventeen-mile traffic jam ensued. Keys residents thought it ridiculous that they had to prove their citizenship to enter the mainland. Key West mayor Dennis Wardlow drove to Federal court in Miami to seek an injunction to stop the roadblock. When he was refused, Mayor Wardlow made an announcement to T.V. crews: "Tomorrow at noon the Florida Keys will secede from the Union!"

True to his word, the next day, the "Conch Republic" was established. Mayor Wardlow was proclaimed Prime Minister of the Republic and immediately declared war on the United States. One minute later, the Republic surrendered to the Union, and applied for one billion dollars in foreign aid.

The "Conch Republic" reared its head again in 1995. This time, organizers went to war with U.S. Navy, throwing Cuban bread and firing water cannons at the 478the Public Affairs Battalion as they "secretly" practiced maneuvers in Key West. This "battle" is reenacted every April during the weeklong "Conch Republic Independence Celebration."

In 2006, the "Conch Republic" attempted to annex an abandoned, disconnected piece of Seven Mile Bridge. A group of Cuban refugees had recently landed there, and the Coast Guard sent them back to Cuba under the "Wet Foot, Dry Foot" policy. The Coast Guard reasoned that the bridge was not connected to land, so did not count as U.S. soil.

MODERN KEY WEST

Many travel advertisements call Key West "paradise". Here, one can spend a day out on the warm, blue water with pods of dolphins swimming by, or on the beach watching flocks of pelicans rise out of the sea. One can enjoy the balmy evening by drinking fine wine and dining on fresh seafood, or laughing with friendly strangers over a bucket of beer in an open-air saloon. People party hard here, but they also know how to kick back and take it easy. It is hard not to be seduced.

On the other hand, "progress" has done big damage to this tiny 2-by-4-mile island. Because of its popularity, Key West has become a small town with big city problems like pollution, traffic, and a large homeless population. The island's natural wonders are feeling the strain. Condos have sprung up where salt ponds once housed rookeries of birds and fish nurseries. Beaches are frequently closed to swimming because of runoff from overwhelmed local sewers. The famed offshore barrier reef—the only one in North America—is dying.

Even as chain stores and chain restaurants slowly take the place of many unique local businesses, Key West stubbornly maintains its appeal. Downtown resembles a year-round carnival, filled with garish colors and oddball sights. "Gypsy" chickens and roosters—decedents of Cuban fighting cocks—run free all over the town, giving the place a laidback, Caribbean feel.

Key West is still relatively free of violent crime (pickpockets and bike thievery are another matter). It is a sophisticated little area, with many fine restaurants, three professional theaters, and its own symphony. It is still a haven for writers, who gather here yearly for the Key West Literary Seminar in January and the Robert Frost Poetry Festival in April. Art galleries are prolific downtown as well, and live music is everywhere, on every corner, booming out into the streets. There is almost never a cover charge to go inside and listen.

Key West's unofficial motto is "One Human Family," and you will see stickers saying so plastered on cars, benches, and mailboxes. The population is a hearty mix of Caucasian, African American, and Latino. Key West also has a large and influential gay, lesbian, and transgender population, with many bars, clubs, and guesthouses catering to gay and lesbian travelers. You needn't be afraid of wandering into a straight bar if you are gay, or a gay bar if you are straight. There is plenty of intermingling, and Key West is famous for its tolerance and "anything goes" attitude.

The local daily newspaper is called *The Citizen*, and it is worth reading just for the "Citizen's Voice" section, where residents kvetch anonymously about chickens and iguanas ruining their gardens, gas prices, or the latest local scandal. Several television stations are devoted to suggesting to the island's guests where to go and what to do: once you arrive, look for KeyTV or Keys Information Station.

A LOCAL'S LIFE

One question many locals are often asked is "What is it like to live in Key West?" Visitors may imagine that locals sit around on the beach all day, have margaritas by the pool every night, and live a laidback lifestyle requiring nothing more that Hawaiian shirts in their wardrobes (only tourists wear these)! Unfortunately, people who move here thinking they will be able to live on permanent vacation are soon disappointed.

Key West is an expensive place to live. Things like food, gas, and household goods are priced higher in the Keys than on the mainland, as they have to be shipped all the way down from Miami or Homestead. Rents and mortgages are high, and space is at a minimum. Houses and apartments are generally small, neighbors live quite close together, and multifloored condos pile as many people as possible into one footprint. Some adventurous folk choose to live aboard their boats, though marina space is tough to come by, and they run the risk of losing their home and all their possessions in one big hurricane.

Key West is home to many people who were born into money or who made their fortune in the Keys' real estate heyday of the 70's and 80's. They often spend their time here doing charity work or involved in the arts community. Many of the Keys' more wealthy inhabitants are "snowbirds"—people who live here only during the part of the year when it is cold elsewhere. Retirees also make up a decent portion of Key West's population. On the other end of the spectrum is the common, working-class Key Wester, who often has to take on two or more jobs just to make ends meet. What kinds of jobs are available in Key West? Most are in the service industry: hotels, restaurants, bars, shops, taxis, and tourist attractions. Alternatively, there is always a call for workers in the medical industry, veterinarians, bankers, accountants, teachers, landscapers, civil servants, and government workers. Key West also seems to have an inordinate amount of lawyers and real estate agents.

Many jobs are seasonal, and, in general, people here count on the money accumulated to during "season" to get them through the "off-season." When there is a hurricane, or even a tropical storm that causes tourists and locals to evacuate, almost everyone in the Keys struggles financially because of the lost hours, wages and tips. To an extent, Key Westers know to help each other out and cut each other slack during active hurricane seasons. But, hurricane or no, the bills will need to be paid and food put on the table.

Ever wonder what it's like to be in Key West during a hurricane? Generally, the mood is calm and collected—though the nightly news certainly tries to create a state of excitement. Almost every local has seen the news crews standing in front of an electric fan and talking about being "battered by the wind." They will find the deepest puddle on the island and stand in it while filming, declaring "Key West is under water tonight!" When the government issues a "mandatory evacuation for residents," the police do not go door-to-door and force residents to leave. Many locals do evacuate during storms, however, many choose to "tough it out" and "hunker down." The government prefers to err on the side of caution, issuing mandatory evacuations days before the path of the hurricane is clear. Often, the storm passes without even touching the Keys. But don't think for a second that Key Westers don't take hurricanes seriously. They know to stay inside, shutter up the house, have plenty of canned goods, bottled water (and beer) and flashlights with fresh batteries.

Despite the drawbacks, most Key Westers agree that the quality of life here is just better than many other places. There's the weather, the water, the arts, and the small-town feeling. After living here a few years, you will be hard-pressed to walk into a bar and not find someone you know. People may even start to call you "Bubba" (a term of endearment for someone who has lived here a long time.) Though true "conchs" are those born in the Keys, after seven years, you may call yourself "a freshwater conch" with pride.

Area Orientation

Key West welcomes visitors year round, whether arriving by car or on a Greyhound Bus from mainland Florida, driving straight down US 1 (also known as the Overseas Highway). Visitors also arrive by plane, landing in a tiny "puddle jumper" at Key West Airport, which drops them off near Smather's Beach in New Town. However you decide to get there, there are certain things to consider while planning what time of year to take your trip.

Hurricane season is, officially, from June through November, though August and September have the worst reputations. Every year, without fail, the Keys evacuate tourists at one point or another, so be prepared to have your vacation possibly cut short because of a storm brewing nearby. If a hurricane does hit, and you somehow haven't left the island, you can expect at least a day without electricity—and everything fun shutting down except a few bars that stay open until the police force them to shut, then open again immediately, with or without electricity (Don's Place on Truman is notorious for this.) In 2005, Hurricane Wilma destroyed Key West with a six-foot storm surge that dumped salt water into houses, car engines, gardens, and freshwater ponds. The property damage was enough to ruin many lives, and the native flora and fauna suffered tremendous blows.

A NOTE ON THIS BOOK'S COVERAGE

This guide will focus on the area of Key West known as, interchangeably, "Downtown" or "Old Town." Specifically, this refers to "main vein" Duval Street and its surrounding streets, plus the nearby Waterfront. No where else in Key West is there so much to see and do in such close concentration. Truthfully, many vacationers never even venture into "New Town." We do encourage exploration of the rest of the island, though, and will point out several off-the-beaten-path attractions.

WHO VISITS KEY WEST?

Key West's tourists are a mixture of cruise ship day-trippers, visitors from "mainland" Florida and, in the winter, vacationers from colder parts of the United States. International travelers are less common but not unheard of. Key West attracts a large number of gay and lesbian tourists year-round. Depending on the time of year, you might also see bikers, or spring breakers, or Hemingway wannabe's. Key West is popular as a wedding destination, and is frequently referred to as the sport fishing capital of the world. Families come here too, though parents should be warned that Key West's seedy, sexy, boozy reputation is well earned, and kids may witness some rather scandalous sights.

TOURIST AREAS

There are many reasons why people visit Key West. Oftentimes, people come to visit the only coral reef in North America. Fishing, snorkeling, and diving are popular pastimes at the reef. Others enjoy boating, jet skiing, kayaking, or any number of water activities offered in Key West. Some come to visit the beach by day and indulge in the nightlife after dark. Some ignore the water altogether and come just for the great bars, live music, and late night revelry. There are also plenty of restaurants, shops, galleries, and museums to while away the time.

OLD TOWN AND NEW TOWN

Key West is generally divided into two distinct areas: Old Town and New Town. New Town, further east, resembles a modern suburb of malls, hotels, and other "comforts" of today. This area literally reflects the "new" developments of the key, and is hard to differentiate between many other small American cities.

However, when traveling west, there is a change as drastic as night to day. Visitors quickly enter what people imagine Key West to be: Old Town, which extends to the far western end of the island. Old Town is a mix of gorgeous old houses with plush yards, and bars, restaurants, galleries, and the like. The nearby Waterfront has bars, restaurants, and boats. It is here where the classic Key West lies.

New Town is the area you'll enter first upon arriving in Key West, which consists of North and South Roosevelt Boulevards all the way down to White Street. North Roosevelt is where you'll find your supermarkets, department stores, the local movie complex, and other assorted strip-mall fare. Condos are king in New Town, and if you choose to stay in one of the hotels up here, your stay will probably be significantly cheaper than in Old Town. Most of Key West's beaches are along South Roosevelt, as is the airport.

DUVAL STREET

Duval Street is the "main drag" of tourism, located deep in Old Town. Lower Duval and Mallory Square is where the cruise ships let off their passengers for tee shirts, ice cream, and lunch at one of the many restaurants. Purchasing something in a store on Duval Street will cost you more than if you bought the same item on one of the neighboring streets. There are plenty of raucous bars, overpriced restaurants, and souvenirs shops on Lower Duval. There are also ubiquitous chain stores like The Gap, Coach, Banana Republic, etc. Upper Duval (heading away from the Gulf of Mexico toward the Atlantic Ocean) is where the gay bars, galleries, and more stylish bars and restaurants reside. It is generally quieter, calmer, and more urbane. The island's most lovely beach, Fort Zachary Taylor, is in Old Town. Most of the other beaches are actually in New Town, surrounded, unfortunately, by little more than condos, hotels, and resorts.

BAHAMA VILLAGE

Petronia is the main strip in Bahama Village within Old Town, where Bahamian settlers once lived (andwhere many of their ancestors still reside.) Much of the area still reflects Bahamian architecture, cuisine and culture. Petronia between Duval and Whitehead street is filled with great restaurants like Blue Heaven, Santiago's Bodega and Columbian Grace, plus quaint shops and galleries. As the official start of Fantasy Fest in October, the "Goombay" festival traditionally fills the streets with Bahamian food, crafts, and music.

KEY WEST'S ARCHITECTURE

Key West's architectural claim to fame is its unique "Conch Houses" built with a mix of influences from the New England and the Bahamas (In fact, many of the houses were actually built in the Bahamas and brought here by ship!) They are typically set on piers, feature sloping metal roofs and roof hatches borrowed from shipbuilding. Louvered shutters protect against hurricanes while wraparound porches and verandas make the best of cooling tropical breezes. Many porches are decorated with ornate wooden lacework called "gingerbread".

SEASONS AND EVENTS

The weather in Key West is mild year-round. The most popular time to come, of course, is when it is winter elsewhere. At the height of winter, the mercury occasionally dips below 70°F, prompting locals to don their sweaters though the tourists are still in shorts and tank tops. Summer can be overbearingly hot in the Keys, with the heat index reaching the low hundreds. Even the shallow waters offshore offer little relief, as water temperatures can be well in the 80s. This is when tourists and locals alike tend to empty out of town. The rainy season is May through October, though the rains tend to come conveniently late at night or early in the morning. Or, an intense afternoon burst of rain will temporary drench town, rarely lasting longer than twenty minutes. Hurricane season is officially June through November. Historically, most hurricanes have occurred between mid-August and mid-October.

WINTER

Though the weather in Key West is mild year-round, the most popular time to come, of course, is when it is freezing elsewhere. At the height of winter, the mercury occasionally dips below 70°F in the Keys, prompting locals to don their sweaters though the tourists are still in shorts and tank tops. During the holiday season, you will be delighted by the many festively decorated homes—Key Westers love their Christmas lights! Fun can be had driving around admiring Christmas lights on a scooter, a bike, or a convertible with the top down knowing your friends back home are freezing. There is even a special nighttime tour on the Conch Train to see the most vulgar displays. The **Key West Literary Seminar** (🖰 *kwls.org*) takes place in January, drawing famous guest speakers and writers from around the country.

NEW YEAR'S EVE

Though there are plenty of ways to ring in the New Year in Key West, most people wind up in one of four places. The average tourist heads either to Sloppy Joe's Bar to watch a conch shell drop or to Schooner Wharf, where they lower a "pirate wench" from the mast of a tall ship. A fun, fiesty crowd takes over upper Duval by the Bourbon Street Pub to watch the drag queen Sushi lowered to the street in a giant stiletto. Artistic types join Key West Burlesque on Sunset Pier for their sexy holiday show and dance party.

SPRING

The rainy season is May through October, though the rains tend to come conveniently late at night or early in the morning. Or, an intense afternoon burst of rain will temporary drench town, rarely lasting longer than twenty minutes. Spring breakers take over Smather's Beach and lower Duval Street throughout April.

SUMMER

Summer can be overbearingly hot in the Keys, with the heat index reaching the low hundreds daily. Even the beaches offer little relief, as offshore water temperatures can rise well in the

80s. This is when tourists and locals alike tend to empty out of town. Lobster-hunting is big in late July. The Keys opens its waters to amateur lobster hunters the last Wednesday and Thursday in July, beginning at 12:01 a.m. on Wednesday and ending at 12:00 midnight on Thursday. During this time, there is no commercial lobster fishing, and properly licensed (saltwater with a lobster stamp) locals and visitors can catch up to six legal-sized spiny lobsters for their personal consumption. The following Saturday, there is a **Lobsterfest** on Duval Street, where restaurants set up booths to serve competing versions of the celebrated crustacean. In August, the Botanical Gardens hosts the annual **A Midsummer Night's Dream Extravaganza** featuring arts, crafts and shows for the kids during the day and solstice-themed art, music and wine for adults at night.

INDEPENDENCE DAY

Key West has fireworks on the 4th of July. They are shot off from the White Street Pier, and are best seen from around Higgs and Rest Beach. Across from the White Street Pier, the rotary sets up grills and sells food and drinks. Or, for a $25 entry fee, head to Casa Marina Resort for the day and enjoy the fireworks from their pristine beach. The Casa has bars, buffets, popcorn and ice cream, plus events for the kids like a bounce house and face painting.

FALL

The leaves do not turn colors in Key West, all stays lush and green. In Key West, Halloween takes place during the day and is stricktly for kids. Grown-ups are too tired out from Fantasy Fest to do much celebrating.

FANTASY FEST

(☎ fantasyfest.com) In late October Key West holds its version
of Mardi Gras or Carnivale, known as Fantasy Fest. These nine
days of free-wheeling, costumed, drunken decadence is the
island's busiest and most bizarre time of year. Each year a silly
theme is declared, and costumes and decorations are supposed
to revolve around these themes. Yearly events include a
Caribbean street fair toga party, pet masquerade, headdress
ball, and "pimp and ho" party—all culminating in a crazy
parade down Duval Street. Nudity and public drunkenness are
generally tolerated during Fantasy Fest, so this is not the time
of year to visit with children or if such things offend you. If
you're planning to attend Fantasy Fest, make hotel reservations
early and expect to pay more.

Area
Orientation

GETTING TO KEY WEST

Despite its remote location as the southernmost connected island of the Florida Keys, Key West is very easy to get to. Its
popularity has made it one of the more accessible vacation
destinations.

BY AIRPLANE

An airplane is the easiest way to get to Key West. The
Key West International Airport *(airport code: EYW* ☎
305.296.5439) is reached by connections in Orlando, Miami,
and Atlanta. Only small planes come into Key West, so don't
expect to take a direct flight from a large airport in New
York City or Chicago. The airport is on S. Roosevelt Blvd.,
where there are car rentals and cabs, plus the bus stops there
frequently. Unless you're staying at one of the resorts along

S. Roosevelt, you'll want to make use of transportation. The airport is not within walking distance of Old Town.

BY CAR

Getting to Key West by car is easy, but it takes some time; there are no expressways between Key West and the mainland (there are smaller roads for over 100 miles). Starting in Key Largo, drive down U.S. 1 (also called Overseas Highway). Key West is at the highway's end!

BY BOAT

The **Key West Express** (☎ *877.243.2378)* is a jet-propelled catamaran that leaves from Fort Myers Beach at 8:30am daily at 8:30 a.m., arriving in Key West at noon. The return shuttle leaves Key West at 6 p.m.. The ride one way is four hours and costs $145.00 round trip for adults. Call ahead for reservations.

WHAT TO PACK

Dress in Key West is generally casual, comfortable, and fit for cool-to-warm or warm-to-hot weather, depending on the season and personal temperature preference. Beachwear is a must. But don't worry too much; most things you may forget can be easily bought. Key West is remote, but not too remote.

GETTING AROUND

First, a note on the "lay of the land" in Key West. Key West is approximately 1½ wide by 3 miles long. As you're coming into Key West on the Overseas Highway, you will enter "Stock Island" just before Key West. Stock Island is, technically, part of Key West (in the same way that Brooklyn is part of New

York City.) This tiny "key" is so close to Key West as to be indistinguishable, though it has a very different character from Key West proper. Stock Island is not generally for the tourists. It consists of commercial fishing fleets, trailer parks, and "affordable" housing. It has a public golf course, the animal shelter, and the Florida Keys Community College. There are a couple of funky, low-key saloons and restaurants (like the Hogfish Bar & Grill and the Rusty Anchor) which claim to embody what Key West USED to be like before tourism drove away the fishing fleets.

"Old Town" basically runs from White and Truman to Mallory Square, and encompasses Bahama Village (the streets around Petronia) as well as the Historic Seaport district. This is, generally speaking, where all the action is. Duval Street is Key West's version of New Orleans' Bourbon Street, and has more bars per block than anywhere else in the Keys. Tee shirt shops, clothing boutiques, restaurants, and stores selling overpriced tourist kitsch are also found in droves along Duval. People getting off the cruise ships by Mallory Square usually spend their whole day ashore just on Duval.

CARS

At first glance, renting a car might seem like the easy and logical way to get around. But remember, you are on a tiny island, only 1.5 by 3 miles, and many of the sights you'll want to see are in the same area anyway. Add to that the fact that parking is both expensive and hard to come by downtown, streets are narrow and crowded, and drinking is a very popular pasttime in Key West, and, you may just want to rethink the whole car scenario.

Good reasons to rent a car might be if you are traveling with small children or someone elderly or disabled. A car can also be great if you want to take day trips to the other Keys. Most of Key West's car rentals are located at the airport, and prices are comparable at all of them. Popular rental companies in Key West include Avis, Dollar, Budget, and Hertz.

ELECTRIC CARS

They're fun, fast, and good for the environment! It may seem strange to see people driving around town in glorified golf carts, but these funny little vehicles make a lot of sense in Key West. They're small enough to squeeze down tight streets, open aired for passengers to enjoy the great weather, and they don't break your bank at the gas tank. Nowhere in Key West does the speed limit surpass 35 miles per hour, so you can pretty much go anywhere in your electric car (though people tend to speed excessively on N. Roosevelt in New Town, so avoid it). They cost upwards of $150 a day, and some can seat up to six people.

Electric cars can be rented in numerous locations around town. Try **Tropicar Inc** *(1300 Duval St.* ☎ *305.294.8136)* or **Conch Electric Cars** *(110 Grinnell St.* ☎ *305.294.0995).*

SCOOTERS

Mopeds, or "scooters" as they're known in Key West, are a great way to get around the island, and are the transportation of choice for many residents. It is easy to find parking for a scooter, three dollars fills the gas tank, and best of all... they're fun! Be warned, though, that scooter crashes are dangerous and often deadly. Riders over sixteen are not required to wear a helmet, and few people in Key West do. Obey all the laws of the road, and don't even think of getting on one of these if you've been drinking. And please, if you're driving a scooter for the first time and feel the need to go very, very slow... pull over and let other drivers pass. Don't forget, not everyone in Key West is on vacation. Scooters ride one person or two, depending on the model, and run anywhere from $30 to $80 a day. Scooters can be rented at **Pirate Scooters** *(401 Southard St.* ☎ *1.877.PIRATE-6* 🖱 *piratescooterrentals.com)*, **Moped Hospital** *(601 Truman Ave* ☎ *866.296.1625* 🖱 *mopedhospital.com)*, and **Paradise Scooter & Bike** *(430 Duval St.* ☎ *305.293.1112* 🖱 *paradisescooterrentals.com)*.

BICYCLES

Key West's nice flat roads and narrow streets invite bike riding, and it is a great way to cruise Duval St. without getting caught in traffic. Never ride at night without bike lights (the cops WILL hassle you) and always obey the laws of the road. Do not ride on the sidewalks—many major streets have designated bike paths for your convenience.

For an especially beautiful bike ride, head to the South side of the island and take the bike path along Atlantic Avenue and S. Roosevelt. You'll get to see the island's beaches, a small nature reserve, the salt ponds, and some nice mangroves. Near the airport, the bike path is higher than the ocean, and if you're paying attention you can sometimes spot baby sharks, barracuda, or stingrays in the water below. Bike rentals are about $12 a day.

KEY WEST CITY BUS

(🖱 **keywestcity.com**) The Key West City Bus is air conditioned, costs only $2, and makes many stops all over the island. Wisely, it does not make its way down Duval, so if that's where you're heading, you'll have to walk a few blocks. Unfortunately, the bus is not the most reliable way to get around. It often comes early, or late, and if you miss it, there may not be another for an hour or more. But, with a little luck and a lot of patience, the bus is a cheap way to get from uptown to downtown and vice versa.

TAXIS

Cabs are ridiculously expensive in Key West, and a ride from one end of the other can easily add up to a twenty dollar bill with a decent tip. But cabs are comfortable, reliable, and the only way to travel safely if you've been drinking into the wee hours. Oh... and some of them are pink! Be prepared to have to share cabs with strangers during especially busy times of the year, like after the Fantasy Fest parade, New Year's Eve, and the 4th of July. Do not expect to "hail" a cab in Key West. You must call, and then wait, for one to come and get you. Companies offering cab service in Key West include **Friendly Cab** (☎ *305.295.5555*) and **Five Sixes Taxi** (☎ *305.296.6666*).

PEDICABS

Want a bike ride through Old Town, but want someone else to pedal? These rickshaw-type pedicabs carry two passengers at a time. Usually driven by friendly individuals, they give a surprisingly comfortable ride. Prices are negotiable on slow nights. Just flag one down on the street if you want to ride. Generally, they stick to the lower Duval Street area.

FOR MORE INFORMATION...

There are numerous websites that are devoted to Key West and vicinity. In particular, the official **Monroe County Tourist Development Council** website (● *fla-keys.com*) has general information about Key West and the entire Florida Keys. Or, you can visit the **Key West Chamber of Commerce Visitor's Center** *(Mallory Square, 402 Wall St.)*.

Area
Orientation

Lodging

There are literally hundreds of hotels, motels, inns, bed & breakfasts, and guesthouses in Key West. We will concentrate on those in the Downtown area, though there are plenty of great places in New Town as well—and things are often cheaper on the less popular side of the island (if you really must stay in New Town—something we don't recommend—consider using a travel website such as Travelocity or Hotels.com). Downtown Key West offers everything from bare-bones chain hotels to high-end resorts. Or, if you like a more intimate setting, bed-and-breakfasts ("B&Bs") pride themselves on making you feel like part of the family. Prices vary greatly according to season. If you plan on coming for **Fantasy Fest**, make your reservations early (some people book rooms a year ahead of time!)—and expect to pay a lot.

Prices: As you'll see, Key West accommodations can be very expensive. Prices in this section range from "$" ($220 or less a night) to "$$$" (over $320 per night).

CHOOSING THE RIGHT PLACE TO STAY

Decide what you want before picking a place to stay: is a pool a priority? Do you want a full, homemade breakfast included, or will a store-bought muffin and a cup of coffee do? If you plan on staying out late, you need to be sure there are no curfews or nighttime quiet hours. If you're bringing children or pets, be sure these are allowed—and if you don't want to be around children or pets, there are plenty of places that don't allow either. Some accommodations are male-or-female only.

Generally, these are for gay and lesbian visitors (a rainbow flag outside means gay-and-lesbian friendly).

Key West offers a mixture of accommodations, from resorts that have their own beaches, pools, bars, restaurants and spas to guesthouses offering simply a bedroom with a common bathroom on each floor. Most places offer some sort of "continental breakfast," which can be anything from home-made waffles to store-bought muffins. Many places have a pool and/or a garden, but some don't.

CAMPING IN THE LOWER KEYS

Camping allows visitors to enjoy the subtropical ecosystem of the Keys without the costs of hotels and resorts. With a short driving distance of Key West, there are a couple of options for camping. Boyd's and Bahia Honda provide public restrooms and other amenities, plus are within driving distance to restaurants, shops and attractions. Campers who wish to really rough it should head to Fort Jefferson in the Dry Tortugas—a pristine wildlife refuge accessible only by boat or plane.

BAHIA HONDA STATE PARK
(Big Pine Key ☎ 305.872.2353
⛫ floridastateparks.org/bahiahonda/) About 37 miles from Key West, Bahia Honda boasts naturally occurring white sand, while the rest of the Keys ships its sand in from the Bahamas. With 524 acres of park including 2.5 miles of beach there is room for snorkeling, swimming, boating and fishing. Bahia Honda has a snack shack and convenience store. Bahia Honda offers three camp sites for tents and two for recreational

vehicles. Many tent sites overlook the water. Some shops and restaurants stand within driving distance. About 7 miles away sits the famous Key Deer Refuge, where you can see the miniature deer, an endangered species that exists no where else in the world.

BOYD'S CAMPGROUND
(6401 Maloney Avenue, Stock Island ☎ 305.294.1465
⬮ boydscampground.com) Just moments outside of Key West, Boyd's caters to tent or r.v. campers in a spacious, family-friendly waterfront park. The park has a private beach, heated pool, game room, grocery store, laundry, wireless internet and tiki bar with a giant television, and several bathhouses. City buses are within walking distance if you don't want to drive in and out of Key West.

DRY TORTUGAS NATIONAL PARK
(☎ 305.242.7700 ⬮ nps.gov/drto) The Dry Tortugas is reachable only by boat or by ferry. This national park provides nesting grounds for numerous species of pelagic bird and pristine waters perfect for snorkeling. Camping at Fort Jefferson is a more primitive and isolated experience than in the state parks. Here, you will have no access to grocery stores, bars, or restaurants. There is no fresh water and no showers. No trash cans are provided anywhere on the island. You need to bring everything with you that you will require, and take everything with you when you leave.

OCEAN VIEWS

The ocean is probably one of the main attractions that brought you to Key West in the first place, so why not get a room Oceanside? Expect to pay more for this kind of proximity to the beach. Or, if you must stay on the water but want to save a few bucks, check out some of the many hotels and resorts in New Town (not listed in this guide.)

DEWEY HOUSE / LA MER
**(1319 Duval St. & 506 South St. ☎ 305.296.5611
📱 lamerhotel.com)** These neighboring, non-smoking, oceanfront hotels have a turn-of-the-century feel and spacious rooms. They are connected by a lush tropical garden with a fountain, towering palms and brightly colored flowers. Guests of La Mer Hotel and Dewey House are welcome to a deluxe Continental breakfast with made to order waffles and afternoon tea served with fresh fruits, imported cheeses and other delights. Wake up and view the beautiful sunrise over the Atlantic Ocean, then spend some leisurely time on the wraparound porch. Laundry service, bike and scooter rentals, and other amenities complete the package. Guests rave about the service and all the personal touches. ($$)

HYATT KEY WEST RESORT
(601 Front St. ☎ 305.809.1234 📱 keywest.hyatt.com) By Mallory Square on the Gulf of Mexico, this high-end resort offers private balconies and all the expected amenities. The on-site restaurant, **Nicola**, has great service, but the food is nothing special—you'll find better fare at the local restaurants. The Hyatt has a private (though unimpressive) beach, a marina,

fitness center, a babysitting service, a turtle pond, and poolside waitstaff. ($$$)

OCEAN KEY RESORT ⊗ Must See!

(0 Duval St. ☎ 800.328.9815 🖰 oceankey.com) This gulfside resort—on the very edge of Duval Street—pampers guests with whirlpool tubs, hand-painted furniture, a pool with an ocean view, an in-house spa and fitness center, and two great restaurants (**Hot Tin Roof** for fine dining, the **Sunset Pier** for a casual bite). Some balconies overlook Mallory Square and are a great place to view Key West's famous sunsets. ($$$)

PIER HOUSE RESORT AND CARRIBBEAN SPA

(1 Duval St. ☎ 305.296.4600 🖰 pierhouse.com) This waterfront resort on the Gulf of Mexico features a very nice, private, white sand beach, tropical garden, koi pond, 24-hour pool, day spa, individually-decorated rooms, an elegant restaurant, and a beachside bar and grill. Locals are known to sneak into the charming, offbeat Chart Room Bar. This very expensive hotel offers a great location and good amenities that many guests find to be worth shelling out extra money for. ($$$)

THE REACH AND CASA MARINA

(1435 Simonton St. ☎ 888.318 4316 🖰 reachresort.com & 1500 Reynolds St. ☎ 888.303 5717 🖰 casamarinaresort.com) These interchangable "sister" resorts (both owned by Waldorf-Astoria) are located just on the edge of Old Town. They have their own private beaches with watersports, gorgeous pools, spas and everything you'd expect from a high-end resort experience. The Reach is a block away from the restaurants and galleries of upper Duval St., while the Casa is closer to Higgs Beach and the White Street Pier. ($$$)

SOUTHERNMOST HOTEL ON THE BEACH
(508 South St. ☎ 305.296.6577

☗ southernmostonthebeach.com) Few hotels downtown can claim to be right on the water—Southernmost Hotel is the least expensive among these. A huge private pier allows guests the best spot to sunbathe on the Atlantic Ocean. All rooms are non-smoking, spacious, and decorated with modern style. Some rooms feature Jacuzzi tubs and balconies, wet bars or mini kitchens. There is a large pool and tiki bar, and Duval Street (the quieter end) is just a block away. The "beach" in the title is South Beach—unfortunately, it is not great for swimming, but is a fantastic place to sunbathe or relax with drink in hand, served at the on-beach restaurant. ($$)

SOUTHERNMOST HOUSE
(1400 Duval St. ☎ 305.296.3141 ☗ southernmosthouse.com)
Built as a private residence in 1896, this guesthouse became a Cuban nightclub called Café Cayo Hueso in the 1930s and 40s. In 1996, a $3 million restoration began to turn it into a 13-room hotel, with a museum on the first floor. Locals are known to frequent the bar by the pool overlooking the ocean, cooing over the domestic bunnies that run loose around the gardens. Guests can enjoy a continental breakfast buffet daily, plus in-room wine, champagne and beverage service upon request. The grounds are a frequent site for weddings and parties, so guests may be disgruntled to find the pool, bar, and gardens closed to them during events. ($$)

THE WESTIN KEY WEST RESORT & MARINA

(245 Front St. ☎ 866.716.8108 ☗ westinkkeywest.com) Located practically on top of lower Duval Street attractions and Mallory Square, the Westin features amenities like oceanfront balconies, in-room spa treatments, pool, babysitting service, restaurants, and a private marina. For an even more exclusive experience, rent a guest cottage out at the Westin's Sunset Key—a luxurious private island just a ten-minute boat ride away from Key West. The Westin is fairly interchangeable with the nearby Hyatt resort. Rooms are decent, service is excellent, and the location is hard to beat if you want to stay close to the touristy action. ($$$)

LOWER DUVAL STREET

If you want to stay right in the heart of the action, Duval Street is the place for you. Hotels, inns, and B&B's on Duval tend to be more expensive, provide less space for the dollar, and require earlier reservations than accommodations in other parts of town. If you plan to travel by foot and party hard, lower Duval Street is the place for you.

CASA 325

(325 Duval St. ☎ 305.292.0011 ☗ casa325.com) Casa 325 offers studio and one and two bedroom suites with hardwood floors, handcrafted queen-size beds and kitchenettes—each uniquely decorated in a tropical island theme—in a historic "Conch Victorian" building. A nice pool and friendly resident cats complete the Key West experience. ($)

CROWNE PLAZA LA CONCHA

(430 Duval St. ☎ 305.296.2991 🖥 laconchakeywest.com) It doesn't get more "in the middle of the action" than the 1920s-style Crowne Plaza. This hotel is the tallest building downtown, and the second floor balconies are by far the best place to enjoy the Fantasy Fest parade. The La Concha has played host to some interesting guests, including royalty and presidents. Hemingway mentions it in one of his novels. Tennessee Williams completed "A Streetcar Named Desire" while in residence. Guests can partake of the pool and pool bar, 24-hour fitness center, laundry service, and a host of luxurious amenities. The Crown Room Pub opens directly onto Duval, serves breakfast, lunch, and dinner, and features nightly entertainment. ($$$)

HEARTBREAK HOTEL

(716 Duval St. ☎ 305.296.5558 🖥 heartbreakhotel.org) This funky hotel caters to gay males and features private kitchens but no pool (guests are encouraged to use the Bourbon Street Pub pool.) It is right in the middle of the "gay" part of Duval Street, where the gay clubs and bars are located. Spring breaker guests are discouraged—and there is a strictly enforced "no visitors" rule. Unfortunately, guests have complained about rude service and a "prison-like" atmosphere. ($)

PEGASUS INTERNATIONAL HOTEL

(501 Southard St. ☎ 305.397.8148 🖥 pegasuskeywest.com) Located just off Duval (but overlooking it), this art deco hotel has 30 rooms. The pool and Jacuzzi are attached to a sundeck overlooking the action on Duval. They serve complimentary coffee in the lobby. General consensus: not bad for a budget hotel in a great location, but nothing to write home about. ($)

SOUTHERN CROSS HOTEL

(326 Duval St. ☏ 305.294.3200 ⬤ southerncrosshotel.com)
This place claims to be the oldest Hotel still in operation in Key West—built in 1898. They offer small rooms with one or two beds, mini-suites, and third floor penthouse suites with balconies. This is a hot spot for Fantasy Fest, what with the oversized balcony, which will hold 100 people, just feet above Duval Street. They don't have many frills, and no pool, but the rooms are clean and you can't beat the price for the location. ($)

OLD CUSTOMS HOUSE INN

(124 Duval St. ☏ 305.294.8507 ⬤ oldcustomshouse.com) All rooms, both studios and suites, include a private entrance, efficiency kitchenette and sitting area, plus private bathrooms with antique, claw-footed tubs. The handcrafted beds are made of extinct Dade County Pine. There is no pool, but there is a quaint café and tiki hut. This inn is right next to the raucous Hog's Breath Saloon, so expect noise late into the night. Unfortunately, the management has a reputation for rudeness—and for raising room rates unexpectedly. ($/$$)

UPPER DUVAL STREET

If you want to be in the heart of Key West but without some of the noise, consider a stay on Upper Duval Street, which offers a slightly quieter experience.

AVALON B&B

(1317 Duval St. ☎ 305.294.8233) Located on the quieter end of Duval, Avalon B&B is a restored Victorian house built in 1895. The Avalon boasts canopy-covered beds, tropical foliage over a small pool, breakfast served on marble-topped tables set up café style on the front porch overlooking Duval Street. Hosts Yvonne and Caroline (and the resident kitties) are friendly and helpful. Parking, however, is a bit scarce. ($)

Lodging

CASABLANCA KEY WEST

(904 Duval St. ☎ 305.296.0815) There was a time when Humphrey Bogart and Ernest Hemmingway used to hang out in the lobby under the tree that grows right through the porch. Unfortunately, many guests complain that this inn has seen better days and is in need of repair. Downstairs is an Irish-style pub called "Bogarts" that serves bar snacks. ($)

DUVAL HOUSE

(815 Duval St. ☎ 305.294.1666 ✆ duvalhousekeywest.com) Most of the seven vintage houses on this property are two-and-a-half story Victorian houses with balconies, banisters and gingerbread trim. The décor is white wicker, rattan, bamboo and light tropical pastels. Antiques and folksy artwork give Key West flavor to many of the guest rooms. Tropical gardens with warm brick walkways, a fishpond, a double-hammock and gazebo tempt visitors to sit back and relax, as do the many chaise lounges by the pool. There are a few suites with kitchens and there is one two-bedroom suite. Duval House was chosen as "…one of the ten most affordable romantic inns in the U.S." by *Vacations Magazine*. Breakfast is served poolside. Children are discouraged, and parking costs extra. ($$)

DUVAL INN

(511 Angela St. ☎ 305.295.9531 🖱 duvalinn.com) Don't let the name fool you—Duval Inn is not located on Duval Street, but a few blocks away in a quieter location. This 19th century conch house has individually decorated rooms. A couple of cheaper rooms require you to share a bathroom. The tropical foliage over the pool and brick sundeck encourages relaxation. They offer "some" parking, and a continental breakfast. ($)

LATEDA GUESTHOUSE

(1125 Duval St. ☎ 305.296.6706) This tiny, gay-friendly guesthouse sits above the raucous drag-cabaret bar and restaurant of the same name. There is a decent pool, the staff is very friendly, and free breakfast is served in the restaurant. Parking is an issue—there isn't much of it. ($)

ORCHID KEY INN

(1004 Duval St. ☎ 305.296.9915) This beautifully renovated boutique hotel offers laidback luxury in the form of marble floors, plasma T.V's, and spa-style bathrooms. The comfy pool area, complete with waterfalls and a hot tub, are open 24 hours. Enjoy complimentary happy hour at the Orchid Bar, free continental breakfast, and free Internet and phone usage. Service here is top-notch and the owners pride themselves on their eco-friendly approach to absolutely everything. ($$)

SOUTHERNMOST POINT GUESTHOUSE

(1327 Duval St. ☎ 305.294.0715 🖱 southernmostpoint.com) In 1885 Cuban cigar maker Eduardo H. Gato, Jr. built this rambling Victorian home on the northwest corner of Duval Street. When he disapproved of the way the sun struck one of his favorite porches, he had the whole structure rolled across the street over logs, pulled by mules, and spun it around to create cool, shady porches. The honeymoon suite is romantically decorated, while the poolside "Ernest Hemingway Room" is decorated with the writer in mind. They have a pool and large Jacuzzi surrounded by palm trees, plus a verandah where continental breakfast is served. Suites and deluxe efficiencies have full kitchens. Wine is complimentary. Some rabbits (escapees from Southernmost House) and cats live here for animal lovers. ($)

Lodging

WICKER GUESTHOUSE

(913 Duval St. ☎ 305.296.4275 ⛫ wickerhousekw.com) Tucked away off the hustle and bustle of Duval, this family owned guesthouse consists of six restored houses spanning an entire block. Standard rooms have the usual amenities, and individually designed "deluxe rooms" offer additional luxuries like a fully equipped kitchen, Jacuzzi tub or "jungle" decor. Two-bedroom accommodations may have private porches or balconies. Guest rooms have no phones to distract you from your vacation. They offer limited, free off-street parking and a complimentary continental breakfast served poolside. The grounds are lushly landscaped, and children will enjoy the historic playhouse. ($)

DOWNTOWN OFF-DUVAL

Classic resort and hotel accommodations abound in Downtown Key West. Don't expect many chain hotels, however—part of the area's charm is its independent, unique accommodations.

The following accommodations, located off Duval Street, offer easy access to downtown, often without Duval Street prices.

ALMOND TREE INN

(512 Truman Ave ☎ 305.296.5415 ☗ almondtreeinn.com) This quaint, quiet inn is known for its courteous service and its gorgeous tropical garden complete with waterfalls and piped-in music. They offer a complimentary continental breakfast and happy hour with beer & wine is served daily under the pavilion. Off-street parking is available to guests, one space per room, at a reduced rate of $5 a day. ($$)

BANYAN RESORT

(323 Whitehead St. ☎ 305.296.7786 ☗ thebanyanresort.com) Named after the breathtaking, gigantic banyan tree in front, this stately, all-suite resort consists of eight Victorian houses. The ultra-thick foliage can lend the place a gloomy air in the evenings (as does the rumor that Mr. Cosgrove, the original owner of the hotel, haunts the gardens), but in the daytime the grounds are truly remarkable, featuring over 200 varieties of flowering plants, fruit trees, climbing vines, fish ponds and waterfalls, plus two pools, picnic areas, a Jacuzzi and tiki bar. This is a prime location, near Mallory Square and lower Duval and not far from the beach at Fort Zachary Taylor. ($$)

BEST WESTERN HIBISCUS

(1313 Simonton St. ☎ 305.294.3763 ☗ bwhibiscus.com) Clean, spacious rooms, a giant pool for the kiddies, and a Jacuzzi for the adults guarantee plenty of bang for your buck. Complimentary breakfast and free parking complete the package. This hotel is located on the "quiet end" of Old Town, so if you want to be right in the action, stay elsewhere. ($$)

BLUE MARLIN HOTEL

(1320 Simonton St. ☎ 305.294.2585 ☏ bluemarlinhotel.com) The Blue Marlin boasts large, clean rooms with standard amenities and a pool, though customers complain that the ambiance is rather lacking. A very basic, store-bought breakfast is served in the lobby, and the pool is a decent size. It is close to South Beach and the Southernmost Point, rather far from Mallory Square and the bars on lower Duval. They have plenty of parking. ($)

EL RANCHO MOTEL

(830 Truman Ave. ☎ 305.294.8700 ☏ elranchokeywest.com) Fifty small but well-kept rooms, a small pool, and a surprisingly beautiful courtyard greet you at this budget hotel. They also offer free parking and complimentary breakfast. Some guests have complained about dirty rooms while others disagree—but many complain about low water pressure in the showers, or not enough hot water. Pets are not allowed. ($)

EQUATOR RESORT

(818 Fleming St. ☎ 305.294.7775 ☏ equatorresort.com) This is a clothing-optional resort for gay men. All rooms are non-smoking, and some have luxuries like wet bars, cathedral ceilings and two-man whirlpool bathtubs. All rooms have Mediterranean tile floors and big, comfy beds with lots of pillows. They offer a very basic breakfast, and daily happy hour by the pool is a great place to meet other guests. Be warned that many guest say this isn't the cleanest of accommodations. ($)

THE GARDENS HOTEL

(526 Angela St. ☎ 305.294.2661 🖳 gardenshotel.com) The Gardens has been named "The Prettiest Hotel In Key West" by The New York Times, called one of 2004's World's Best Places to Stay by Conde Nast, and is listed in the book 1,000 Places to See Before You Die. It was once the Peggy Mills Botanical Garden, and the main structure dates back to 1870. Now, enjoy the gardens on winding brick footpaths. There is also a pool with a bar. Standard accommodations feature private entrances, outdoor verandahs, and marble baths—most with Jacuzzi tub, and complimentary breakfast. Travelers compliment the helpful and interesting staff and the friendly, comfortable atmosphere. Children are not permitted. ($$)

MARQUESA HOTEL ⭐ Must See!

(600 Fleming St. ☎ 305.292.1929 🖳 marquesa.com) The Marquesa is a compound of four buildings set around a lush interior garden with a fountain, two swimming pools, and a waterfall. Its transformation from 1884 "conch" houses to beautifully restored rooms and suites, marble baths and superior amenities has brought the hotel the *AAA Four Diamond* award for about two decades. A continental breakfast is brought to your room or served poolside. No smoking in the rooms, pets, or children under fourteen. The adjoining restaurant, Marquesa Café, is one of the most lauded in Key West. ($$$)

THE PALMS HOTEL

(820 White St. ☎ 305.294.3146 🖰 palmshotelkeywest.com)
The Main House was built in 1889 and features lace-like
gingerbread trim and large wraparound verandahs. Adjacent
to the Main House is the recently added two-level guest wing
with rooms decorated with a Caribbean influence, featuring
French doors opening onto a secluded, lushly planted courtyard with a heated swimming pool and tiki bar, surrounded by
a sunbathing deck. Pets are allowed, but spring breakers are
discouraged, as there is a "no noise policy" during the over-
night hours. Some guests have claimed that service is sketchy
here, and the whole place is becoming a bit run-down, while
others are willing to overlook those facts for the great price. ($)

SIMONTON COURT HISTORIC INN AND COTTAGES

(320 Simonton St. ☎ 305.294.3200 🖰 simontoncourt.com) This
two-acre, private compound consists of the two-story Inn,
Manor House, Townhouse Suites, The Mansion, six cottages
and four pools. The Inn was once a cigar factory. A brick
walkway, once a lane, runs past the pools and historic cottages
built in 1880 as the homes of cigar factory workers. Today this
lane is a footpath through the stunning gardens. Each cottage
offers a porch and private patio. The Inn, Manor House,
Townhouse and The Mansion offer a variety of suites and
guest rooms. Many have private porches or sundecks and some
have Jacuzzis. Complimentary breakfast is served poolside.
Children are not welcome. ($$$)

SPANISH GARDENS MOTEL

(1325 Simonton St. ☎ 305.294.1051) This family-operated
motel has a pool and a grocery store right across the street.

They have a reputation for being hospital and affordable, with small but clean rooms. Located on the quiet end of old town, it is a decent walk to Mallory Square and the Duval Street bars. Spring breakers are discouraged. ($)

WESTWINDS INN

(914 Eaton St. ☎ 305.296.4440 ⬇ westwindskeywest.com)
Located in the historic seaport/waterfront area, Westwinds has two small pools and a beautifully landscaped tropical garden. All rooms are non-smoking, and televisions are limited to rooms in only one of its five buildings. The lounge offers television, wireless Internet access, library and refrigerator. Complimentary breakfast is served on the poolside deck. The only parking available is at the pricey public garage across the street. The Westwinds is just two blocks away from lower Duval, and is right next to several restaurants, lively bars, and charter boats. Children under twelve are not allowed. ($)

BED & BREAKFASTS, GUESTHOUSES

Key West is particularly famous for its guesthouses. But what is the difference between a guesthouse and a standard hotel or inn? Generally, guesthouses and bed-and-breakfasts offer a more intimate experience than hotels and inns. The owner usually lives on the premise, and they pride themselves on making you feel like "family".

ALEXANDER PALMS COURT

(715 South St. ☎ 305.296.6413) This tropical compound-style guesthouse offers comfortable, spacious accommodations ranging from standard rooms to full suites with kitchens in

1950s-style decor. Stately palms and picturesque landscaping surround a lagoon-style pool. A rudimentary breakfast is complimentary. Guests enjoy being two blocks away from Duval, but far enough away to enjoy peace and quiet. ($)

AMBROSIA HOUSE TROPICAL LODGING & AMBROSIA HOUSE TWO ⭐ Must See!
(615 & 618 Fleming St. ☎ 305.296.9838

⛙ ambrosiakeywest.com) This private compound consists of six restored buildings nestled among nearly two acres of tropical landscaping. Guests enjoy one of the three pools, or visit Nancy Forester's Secret Garden right next door. Rooms and suites have private entrances, many with French doors opening onto verandas, courtyards, and patios. Rooms display original work by Keys artists, wicker or wood furniture, and spacious bathrooms. The honeymoon suites feature 4-poster canopy beds and in-room Jacuzzis. Townhouses and a stand-alone cottage are also available. They offer a complimentary breakfast, parking, and are child and pet friendly. ($)

ANDREWS INN
(0 Whalton Ln ☎ 305.294.7730 ⛙ andrewsinn.com) This tiny inn is in the backyard of the Hemingway House, and you can expect to see some of Key West's famous six-toed cats prowling the yard. Guest rooms are named for settings in Hemingway's books, such as "Pamplona" and "Paris", and feature wicker furniture, tropical decor, and unique artwork. Lush gardens and a pool compliment champagne continental breakfast and evening cocktails. They also offer cottages in the form of Bahama-style homes with outside patios or terraces

and Jacuzzis. Children and pets are not accommodated at the inn, but are accepted in the cottages. ($)

ANGELINA GUESTHOUSE

(302 Angela St. ☎ 305.294.4480 ✆ angelinaguesthouse.com)
Once a 1920s bordello and gambling spot, the Angelina prides itself on rooms without television or radio and a friendly but unobtrusive staff. The heated lagoon-style pool surrounded by foliage entices guests to lounge in a hammock by the waterfall. Rooms vary, some share bathrooms, but all are quaint and clean, if somewhat small, and well worth the affordable price. A homemade breakfast is served each morning—don't miss the oven-fresh cinnamon buns. No one under 21 is allowed. ($)

ARTIST HOUSE

(534 Eaton St. ☎ 305.296.3977 ✆ artisthousekeywest.com)
This restored Victorian mansion features elegant, antique-filled rooms—guests say it's like stepping back in time. The architecture is Colonial Queen Ann style, with numerous graceful columns, verandas and gingerbread, and a magnificent turret. The Artist House has been featured on The Discovery Channel, A&E Television, Good Morning America, and other national spots. Breakfast is served by the L-shaped pool. ($$)

AUTHORS GUESTHOUSE

(725 White St. ☎ 305.294.7381 ✆ authorskeywest.com) Authors were "conceived to honor the literary masters who lived and worked in quaint, colorful Key West." Each room in this compound of historic Conch-style houses, suites, and rooms is named after an author who lived in Key West. A continental breakfast is served by the small pool in the very nice garden and courtyard. Pets are not welcome, nor are spring breakers, but kids under 16 stay for free. This is on a busy street, so be prepared to deal with some noise. ($)

BIG RUBY'S GUESTHOUSE

(409 Appleruth Ln. ☎ 305.296.2323 🖱 bigrubys.com) This gay & lesbian, clothing-optional guesthouse is smack in the middle of the action, just off of mid-Duval. "Unlimited" Happy hour is served nightly, and breakfast, served by the pool, is made to order. There is a giant hot tub, a gym and on-site bike rentals. Big Ruby's attracts an international crowd, but most of the clientele is gay and lesbian couples. ($$$)

BLUE PARROT INN

(916 Elizabeth St. ☎ 305.296.0033 🖱 blueparrotinn.com) Built in 1884, this restored Bahamian-style guesthouse features nine guest units, each with its own distinctive decor. Watch the resident cats goof off on the sundeck all day while lounging by the pool or in the garden. The garden's centerpiece is a stunning staghorn fern strung along branches of a gumbo limbo tree. A continental breakfast is served poolside daily. No kids or pets are allowed, and spring breakers are discouraged. ($)

CHELSEA HOUSE

(709 Truman Ave ☎ 305.296.6558) This establishment was formerly two different guesthouses (one being the Red Rooster Inn). Expect clean rooms, a pool with a sundeck, nice gardens, and a porch facing busy Truman Ave. where breakfast is served. The staff is always helpful, and pets are okay. ($$)

CENTER COURT HISTORIC INN

(915 Center St. ☎ 305.296.9292 🖱 centercourtkw.com) The child-and-pet friendly Center Court consists of the main guesthouse (constructed in 1874) surrounded by cigar-makers' cottages. Rooms are stocked with beach bags, beach towels, and other amenities. The heated pools are surrounded by lush foliage, whirlpools, and a clothing-optional sundeck. Aviaries filled with cockatiels complete the experience. ($$$)

COCOPLUM INN

(615 Whitehead St. ☎ 305.295.2955 🖱 cocopluminn.com) Built in 1891, Cocoplum offers spacious accommodations with antique furnishings—different in every room. The complimentary breakfast is prepared to order by a professional chef, and the pool area is lovely and well-kept. ($$)

CONCH HOUSE HERITAGE INN

(625 Truman Ave. ☎ 305.294.8700 🖱 conchhouse.com) This charming two-story home offers luxurious accommodations in one of the island's earliest historic family estates. Restored in 1993, The Conch House features Victorian styling with Bahamian influences: high ceilings, wood shutters, wraparound spindled porches and picket fences. Guests can choose from rooms in the main house, furnished with individually selected antiques, the Caribbean-style wicker rooms in the garden poolside cottage, or the cozy poolside cabana. They also offer complimentary breakfast, a pool, and bike rentals. ($)

CORAL TREE INN & OASIS GUESTHOUSE

(821 & 822 Fleming St. ☎ 305.292.2131) These two males-only, clothing-optional hotels share amenities. Coral Tree

Inn offers eleven rooms with private balconies and a pool surrounded by roman columns. Breakfast is complimentary, as is wine and hors d'oeuvres at sunset. The Oasis boasts a 24-man jet Jacuzzi, and complimentary frozen drinks are served at poolside every afternoon at 3 p.m. The clientele at both inns tend toward middle-aged. ($)

CURRY HOUSE

(806 Fleming St. ☎ 305.294.6777 ☗ curryhousekeywest.com)
This historic home was built by ship builders on Green Turtle Cay in the Bahamas, shipped to Key West, and assembled in 1889! Each room at the historic Curry House is unique. Most have queen-sized poster beds and at least one door that opens onto a veranda or wraparound porch. There are quiet nooks around the house and on the porches where you can sit and look out over the pool, or watch people strolling down Fleming Street. Amenities include a homemade breakfast, complimentary happy hour by the pool. No children under 13, and no pets, except the company of neighborhood cats. Guests say the staff makes you feel like family, and love that the pool is open 24 hours and artistically lit at night. ($)

CURRY MANSION INN

(511 Caroline St. ☎ 305.294.5349 ☗ currymansion.com) This sister B&B to Curry House dates from 1899, and offers similar amenities with its 28 elegant, romantic rooms. Most open onto a sparkling pool and hot tub and the lush foliage of the Curry Estate—but other rooms overlook such eyesores as the parking lot or an empty courtyard on another property. The room feature wicker furniture and handmade quilts. Pets are welcome here. ($$)

CYPRESS HOUSE

(601 Caroline St. ☎ 305.294.6969 🖱 cypresshousekw.com) Built in 1888, this Grand Conch mansion is a great example of Bahamian architecture. Old fashioned porches, lush tropical gardens and secluded sunbathing around a 40' heated lap pool all add to the enjoyment of your stay, as does complimentary hot breakfast and the best free cocktail hour on the island with a full bar and hot and cold snacks. Each room is different, some with one king or one queen bed, others have two queen beds. Furniture styles vary from wicker to an eclectic mix of antiques. Some have private verandahs or outside sitting areas. Lots of extra amenities & personal touches, lovely gardens, and the inn's resident cats and dogs keep customers coming back. ($$)

DUVAL GARDENS

(1012 Duval St. ☎ 305.292.3379 🖱 duvalgardens.com) Small but clean rooms are cutely decorated and beds have romantic netting. The second floor boasts a wraparound balcony overlooking Duval Street. There is a tiny lap pool, and, strangely given the name, no gardens. Complimentary continental breakfast Buffet is served each morning. ($)

EDEN HOUSE

(1015 Fleming St. ☎ 305.296.6868 🖱 edenhouse.com) Eden House offers a heated pool, Jacuzzi, elevated sundeck, waterfalls, hammocks, swings, and a garden cafe. Luxury suites, private, and semi-private rooms are available. Children are welcome (but pets are not), all buildings are non-smoking, and rooms have no clocks or radios by design. There is no complimentary breakfast, but there is a free happy hour. Downstairs features an excellent upscale, on-site restaurant called Azur. The staff is fun and friendly. ($)

THE GRAND

(1116 Grinnell St. ☎ 305.294.0590

⛟ thegrandguesthouse.com) Built in the 1880s, The Grand was a rooming house for workers at a nearby cigar factory. Now, guests enjoy the beautiful terraced garden with several seating areas and a fresh, plentiful breakfast on the patio. The Grand is recipient of the Superior Florida Keys Lodging award, and is widely known to be one of the best accommodation bargains in Key West Some rooms have kitchenettes. No children under 12 or pets allowed. ($)

HERON HOUSE

(512 Simonton St. ☎ 305.294.9227 ⛟ heronhouse.com) This restored hotel features beautiful detailing like stained glass and fine woodwork in each of its 23 rooms. Guest can explore their collection of exotic orchids or take a dip in the pool surrounded by lush greenery. Guests wake up to a complimentary continental breakfast and top off the evening with a wine and cheese tasting on weekends, compliments of the innkeepers. No one under 21 allowed. ($$)

HERON HOUSE COURT

(412 Frances St. ☎ 800.932.9119 ⛟ heronhousecourt.com) Built circa 1900, this converted residence features 16 comfortable rooms and suites, all decorated in unique styles inspired by the tropical atmosphere of South Florida. Touches like hand-crafted furniture, stained glass, and local artwork add to the charm of each room. Guests can enjoy a soak in the hot tub or mingle at the complimentary weekend happy hour. Suites at Heron House Court have private decks. ($$)

ISLAND HOUSE

(1129 Fleming St. ☎ 305.294.6284 📞 islandhousekeywest.com) This gay men's clothing-optional resort offers a large heated pool and Jacuzzis that are open 24 hours a day, a health club with a gym and spa area with sauna and steam room, a café serving three meals poolside, tiki bar, free happy hour and a 24-hour erotic video lounge. Rooms are decorated in a masculine motif inspired by Ernest Hemingway's home in Havana. You know you're in a sexy place when a 24-hour "adult entertainment" channel is complimentary in every room. ($$)

KEY LIME INN

(725 Truman Ave ☎ 305.294.5229 📞 keylimeinn.com) The estate buildings in this 37-room historic hotel originally date from 1854 to 1949. Great landscaping surrounds a large pool, and there is on-site parking. Accommodations are tailored to couples, with most all rooms providing either a queen or king-size bed. Guests have complained that the continental breakfast, served poolside, was lacking, and that the rooms' decor lack charm. Pets are not allowed. ($)

KEY WEST BED & BREAKFAST: THE POPULAR HOUSE

(415 William St. ☎ 305.296.7274) You can share a bathroom for a lower price, or have your own for a higher price. Either way, you'll get a great price for spacious, comfy rooms, friendly service, and an abundant breakfast. The decor is colorful and eclectic with local artwork on display, and the giant Jacuzzi is a terrific place to unwind. ($)

L'HABITATION GUESTHOUSE

(408 Eaton St. ☎ 305.293.9203 🖱 lhabitation.com) Built circa 1874, L'Habitation's architecture displays Victorian and Bahamian accents. Guests enjoy a continental breakfast on the terrace. All rooms are non-smoking, pets are not allowed, nor are children under 12. There is no pool, but the price is right if you want to stay close to the action on lower Duval without shelling out big bucks. ($)

LIGHTHOUSE COURT

(902 Whitehead St. ☎ 305.294.9588 🖱 lighthousecourt.com) This was once a notorious gay guesthouse, famous for its parties. In 2004, it changed hands and went "respectable". Buildings in this historic compound of ten conch houses date from 1890 to the 1920s. Accommodations are tailored to couples. Rooms are non-smoking, and open out onto a porch, deck, or courtyard. A few "budget" rooms are available if you're willing to share a bathroom. The half-acre gardens feature porches, brick paths, tree swings, hammocks, chaise lounges, a sundeck, and the pool deck. And yes, there is a lighthouse. There is a fitness center free to use for guests, and a tiki bar/café by the pool. Complimentary breakfast is served daily in the courtyard. Some of the rooms lack good views. Also, some guests have complained about rude service and old mattresses. ($)

MANGO TREE INN

(603 Southard St. ☎ 305.293.1177 🖱 mangotree-inn.com) Built in 1858, Mango Tree Inn is a Bahamian style mansion featuring Dade County pine (now extinct) floors and walls, crown moldings, and a unique octagonal wing. It sits under a wild orchid tree on Southard Street, just one block from Duval Street. Upper and lower porches under a tin roof overlook a large heated pool and garden deck. Some rooms have kitchens, and all have funky, tropical decor. The owners' pet parrots add a touch of the tropics to the garden. ($$)

MARRERO'S GUEST MANSION

(410 Fleming St. ☎ 305.292.1929 🖰 marreros.com) Built in 1889 by Francisco Marrero, this hotel comes with a resident ghost—Marrero's bride for whom the house was built. It also features a clothing-optional pool area, tropical gardens, in-room honor bar, outdoor shower, complimentary breakfast, and evening cocktail hour. Guests compliment the tranquil atmosphere created by the friendly husband-and-wife owner and their small staff. All rooms are non-smoking. No pets or people under 21 are allowed. ($)

MERLIN GUESTHOUSE

(811 Simonton ☎ 305.296.3336 🖰 merlinguesthouse.com) This 20-room hotel, built in 1930, has had a colorful past, varying from respectable rooming house to bordello and flophouse. Rooms are cozy and rustic, and a continental breakfast is served poolside each morning. Rooms are non-smoking and they do not accommodate pets. Guests are on their own when it comes to finding parking. ($)

THE MERMAID AND THE ALLIGATOR

(729 Truman Ave ☎ 305.294.1894 🖰 kwmermaid.com) This 1904 Victorian home offers a full breakfast and a lovely little pool surrounded by a beautiful courtyard (the owner is a landscaper and horticulturist). Complimentary wine at sunset and friendly resident dogs add to the inn's vibrant personality. Each room has its own decor, some with private balconies, marble showers, French doors or exposed beam cathedral ceilings. Children or pets are not permitted. ($$)

NASSAU HOUSE

(1016 Fleming St. ☎ 305.296.8513 📖 nassauhouse.com) Fun tropical decor and a gorgeous lagoon-style pool and Jacuzzi are the main attractions here. Breakfast is complimentary, as is pre-sunset wine and snacks. Husband-and-wife team Bo and Letty are known to make guests feel like family. Guests call this place a "gem" and say it is truly one of Key West's few great bargains. ($)

OLD TOWN MANOR

(511 Eaton St. ☎ 305.294.2170 📖 oldtownmanor.com) Formerly "Eaton Lodge," the building is circa 1886 found new owners in fall of 2006. The new innkeepers redecorated each room individually and according to the doctrines of feng shui. They have begun restoration of the garden—one of the oldest in Key West—to its original historic beauty, and will include a fish pond and swimming pool. A healthy, environmentally friendly, homemade, organic breakfast is complimentary, as are free DVD rentals. Pets are allowed in certain rooms. All rooms are smoke-free, and spring breakers are not welcome. There is parking for motorcycles and mopeds only. ($)

PARADISE INN

(819 Simonton St. ☎ 305.293.0807 📖 theparadiseinn.com) Guests stay in renovated one and two bedroom "cigar makers" cottages. Additional suites are located in two authentically reproduced Bahamian-style houses with vine covered porches, sundecks and shaded balconies. The decor emphasizes light oak, natural fibers and marble with shades of beige and gold, functional furnishings, and subtle botanical prints. French doors open wide to let in the Key West sunshine. Limestone and brick paths meander through the spacious grounds, landscaped with tropical flora. There is a large, fountain-fed pool, Jacuzzi, and koi pond. Breakfast is served in the lobby. All rooms are nonsmoking and pets are not allowed. Guests say this place truly is "paradise", with immaculate rooms and an attentive staff. ($$)

PEARL'S RAINBOW

(525 United St. ☎ 305.292.1450) The main building at Pearl's Rainbow was originally a Marrero cigar factory built in the late 1800's. Once a clothing-optional resort for lesbians, Pearl's now opens its doors to men as well. Pearl's has 38 rooms and suites at a variety of prices. It offers two heated pools, two hot tubs, a restaurant and bar (often attended by local women) and poolside bar, all at the quieter end of Old Town. Pearl's includes a light complimentary breakfast. Rooms are rather modest, but the great price and greater atmosphere make up for lack of space. ($)

PILOT HOUSE

(414 Simonton St. ☎ 305.294.8719 🖱 pilothousekeywest.com) Pilot House is a two-story Victorian Mansion built circa 1900 by Julius Otto as his private home, boasting fireplaces, verandas and porches with hand-milled spindles and gingerbread trim. Rooms come with marbled baths and fully equipped kitchens.

A clothing optional pool and spa complete the experience.
Bikes are rented out at the front desk. ($)

WEATHERSTATION INN

(57 Front St. ☎ 305.294.7277) This Bahama-style inn has eight
distinctly styled guest rooms plus several balconies and decks
all looking out on the tropical landscaping and a private pool.
Complimentary breakfast, free parking, and lots of amenities
add to this B&B's quiet appeal. The inn is within short walking
distance of Fort Zachary Taylor—the most beautiful beach on
the island—plus lots of great bars and restaurants. ($$)

Area Attractions

First things first. Key West is a small island, but filled with a lot to see and do! This section explores many of the island's attractions. As you'll see, there is so much packed into such a small place, so don't expect to see and do everything.

TOURS OF KEY WEST

Though Key West is a small island, there is a certain amount of confusion involved in getting around. The streets are in no par-ticular order and sometimes change names in the middle. In New Town, suddenly, there are several numbered streets—then there is a huge section of Old Town with similar-sounding women's first names (Olivia, Amelia, and Louisa for example.) There are many tiny lanes no bigger than alleyways, then a cou-ple of giant, curved boulevards going around the edges of the island. A guided tour is a fun, interesting way to see the island, get your bearings, and learn things you might not have known otherwise.

CITYVIEW TROLLEY TOURS

(☎ 305.294.0644 🖱 cityviewtrolleys.com/keywest) CityView is a new company in Key West, and their trolley fleet just hit the streets of Key West in 2010. CityView's narrated tour features nine pick up locations including Clinton Square, Higgs Beach, Key West Bight, Florida Keys Eco-Discovery Center, and Duval Street. Jump on or off at will all day for $19, $8 for kids. Trolleys run every 30 minutes from 9:30 a.m. to 4:30 p.m.

THE CONCH TOUR TRAIN

(☎ 305.294.5161 ▮ conchtourtrain.com) Celebrating the famous train built by Henry Flagler that first brought tourists onto the island, the Conch Train is an unmistakable sight in downtown Key West. Picture a giant, old-fashioned toy choo-choo big enough to carry over fifty passengers through the streets daily. Tours last about an hour and costs $29 per adult, $14 for kids under 12. Kids under 4 ride free. The train departs every 30 minutes, and can be boarded at three spots all quite close together on Front Street, Mallory Square, or Flagler Station. The emphasis of the tour is historical as well as commercial (some businesses pay to have conductors point them out on the tour). Kids love it. Locals who get stuck driving behind the slow-moving trains have been known to give passengers a spe-cial wave, consisting of one or two fists, or occasionally a single finger. Just smile and wave back. Remember, you're on vacation, while they're probably late to work.

GHOSTS AND GRAVESTONES

(☎ 305.294.4678 ▮ ghostsandgravestones.com/key-west) The newest ghost tour in Key West differs slightly from the others in that it begins on board a trolley and heads into New Town to a few locations where the walking-only ghost tours don't travel. For example, this tour brings visitors to the Grotto of our Lady of Lourdes, the African Slave Cemetery and finally, a civil war fort to meet with the famous Robert the Haunted Doll. The nightly tour lasts an hour and a half at a cost of $30. This tour is not recommended for children under 13.

ISLAND CITY STROLLS

(☎ 305.294.8380 ⬙ seekeywest.com/walk.htm) Local writer Sharon Wells offers private tours catering to each particular group's inter-ests. The tours are sometimes by foot, sometimes by bike, always an intimate and interesting experience. Samples of recent tours include a Literary Landmarks tour, a Duval Street tour (with plenty of stops for "refreshments") and an Alluring Houses and Gardens tour. Wells' tours require reservations two days in advance. Call for current times and departures. Please note these tours only operate during the "season" (approx. Oct.-July.)

KEY WEST GHOST TOUR

(☎ 305.294.9255 ⬙ hauntedtours.com) Eccentric guides lead this lan-tern-lit, nighttime stroll around town in Victorian era, gothic garb. Tours depart nightly, rain or shine, at 8 p.m. and 9 p.m. from the lobby of the La Concha Hotel on Duval. Tickets are $18 per adult, $13 per child. The tour lasts 90 minutes, and reservations are required. Key West is chock-full of ghoulish legends and tales of true hauntings—and you might just get a history lesson in the process. Cameras and video recorders are encouraged to try to catch "para-normal activity" on tape! This tour is child-friendly (no actors jump out at you, there are no staged events). Key West Ghost Tour—the "original"—has been featured on shows like *America's Most Haunted Places* and *Weird Travels.*

KEY WEST GHOSTS AND LEGENDS HAUNTED TOUR

(☎ 305.294.1713 ⬙ keywestghosts.com) Apparently, there are enough creepy places in Key West to support two ghost tour companies conducting walking tours at the same time.

This one leaves from the Porter Mansion Courtyard. Adult tickets are $18, chidren $10. The tour lasts 90 minutes and covers about one mile by foot. Learn about haunted Victorian mansions, island pirate lore, voodoo superstitions and rituals, and a Count who lived with the corpse of his beloved. Reservations are required.

LLOYD'S ORIGINAL TROPICAL BIKE TOUR

(☎ 305.294.1882) See Key West through the eyes of a 30-year Key West veteran. Biking is fun and easy in Key West—the streets are flat, and many roads provide bike paths or lanes. Bikers meet at Truman Avenue And Simonton Street. Lloyd prefers showing off the natural, noncommercial side of Key West at a leisurely pace, stopping on back streets and in back-yards of private homes to sample native fruits and view indigenous plants and trees. Stops include the City Cemetery and the Medicine Garden, a private meditation garden. The tours run 90-120 minutes and cost $20, plus $3 for bike rental.

KEY WEST HOUSE AND GARDEN TOUR

(☎ 305.294.9501 🖰 oirf.org) These tours through private historic homes and personal gardens happen at various times throughout the year. Advance tickets are not required, and are $25 per person. Proceeds benefit the Old Island Restoration Foundation. See the houses on your own, or jump in the Conch Tour Train that takes visitors to all houses on the tour.

OLD TOWN TROLLEY TOURS

(☎ 305.296.6688 🖰 trolleytours.com) The orange and green trackless "trolley" is owned by the same company as the Conch Train and prices are the same. But the trolley moves a little faster, goes a little further, and has many more off/on stops. If you want to explore an area in depth, you can simply get off and board another trolley later. The tour itself lasts about ninety minutes.

MUSEUMS

Key West is proud of its colorful history and famous inhabitants. Once tourism firmly took hold, huge restoration and preservation projects began to insure that the island's past would always be close at hand. Apart from many historic private homes, Key West has several historic buildings open to the public, many housing genuine antiques, artifacts, and memorabilia from days past. Some, like the Hemingway Home, are constantly bustling with tourists. Others are smaller, quieter, and offer a more intimate glimpse of the island's history.

AUDUBON HOUSE & GARDENS

(205 Whitehead St. ☎ 305.294.2116 ⬤ audubonhouse.com) This historic house celebrates naturalist John James Audubon, who resided in Key West in the 1830s. 28 first-edition lithographs of Audubon's drawings are on display, as are antiques reminiscent of Captain John Gieger, the wrecker who built and lived in the house with his family. Audio tours are available (in the voices of actors portraying the Giegers) as are written tours. Adults pay $10 to enter, children $5. Unfortunately, not many artifacts actually pertain to Audubon, nor were many of the antiques actually owned by the Giegers.

CURRY MANSION INN

(511 Caroline St. ☎ 305.294.5349 🍷 currymansion.com) Built in 1905 by Milton Curry, Florida's first self-made millionaire, the inn's public rooms display antiques and memorabilia, the highlight being a very nice 1899 billiards table. The view of Key West Harbor from the "widow's walk" is amazing. It costs $5 to look around.

EAST MARTELLO MUSEUM

(3501 S. Roosevelt Blvd. ☎ 305.296.3913 🍷 kwahs.com/martello.htm) Swing out to New Town to explore this 1862 Civil War brick for-tress overlooking the Atlantic. Part historical museum filled with interesting artifacts from Key West's past, and part Key West gal-lery, the East Martello is also the home of famous "Robert," the haunted doll, who supposedly moves of his own accord on occa-sion. The works of folk-artists Mario Sanchez and Stanley Papio are on display downstairs—they're okay, but seem out of place within the formidable fortress. Admission is $6 for adults, $3 for children.

FORT ZACHARY TAYLOR ✪ Must See!

(End of Southard St., Truman Annex ☎ 305.292.6713 🍷 fortzacharytaylor.com) Within Fort Zachary Taylor Historic State Park sits this citadel built in 1866 to defend the coastline. The fort played major roles in the Civil War and the Spanish-American War. Today, it houses many genuine artifacts like cannons and cannonballs, and is the site of yearly Civil War re-enactments and a haunted house at Halloween. The fort itself is a marvel of engineering, with sanitary facilities flushed by the tide and a desalination plant that produced drinking water from the sea. Entrance to the park is paid according to how many people are in the vehicle: $4.50 per person with just one in the car—the more people in the car, the less that you pay per person. Pedestrians and bicyclists pay $2.50. On site is also the most beautiful beach on the island.

HEMINGWAY HOME & MUSEUM
(907 Whitehead St. ☎ 305.294.1136 🖰 hemingwayhome.com)
"Papa" Ernest Hemingway resided here from 1931-1939, and wrote several of his most famous works while in residence, including *For Whom the Bell Tolls*, *The Green Hills of Africa*, and *To Have and Have Not*. Built by wrecker Ava Tift in 1851, the house was extensively re-modeled and redecorated by Pauline Hemingway—who fitted her backyard with the island's first residential swimming pool. First editions of Hemingway's works and photos from throughout his life are on display. Many of the actual furnishings of the house are still intact—though many others are replicas.

Much ado is made about the 6-toed cats that roam the property, the "descendants" of Papa's pets. Ernest Hemingway had a particular fondness for a special kind of cat—one with six toes. These polydactyl cats, or "six-toed"cats, are now more famously known as Hemingway Cats. They roam the city, but are mostly found in and around the Hemingway House, and (of course) they grace many a postcard. Admission is $11 for adults, $6 for children.

HARRY S. TRUMAN LITTLE WHITE HOUSE
(111 Front St. ☎ 305.294.9911 🖰 trumanlittlewhitehouse.com)
President Harry S. Truman began spending time in Key West in 1946 under orders from his doctors. He spent 11 working vacations in the "Little White House." Built in 1890, the house

was renovated for Truman in 1948. The rooms have been restored to exactly how they looked in Truman's day, and there is also a collection of photos and other presidential memorabilia. There is also a "presidential gift shop" for real Truman fans. Admission is $11 for adults, $5 for kids.

HERITAGE HOUSE MUSEUM

(410 Caroline St. ☎ 305.296.3573 ☗ heritagehouse.com) The vintage memorabilia celebrates socialite Jessie Porter, whose lauded guests included Tallulah Bankhead, Thorton Wilder, and Gloria Swanson to name a few. Robert Frost wintered in the small cottage in the rear garden between 1945 and 1960. The main reason to go, though, is to sit in the garden and listen to recordings of Frost reading his poetry. Sometimes, you can catch a local writers' groups meeting here for just this purpose. Cost is $6 for adults, $1 for kids.

KEY WEST SHIPWRECK HISTORIUM MUSEUM

(1 Whitehead St. ☎ 305.292.8990 ☗ shipwreckhistoreum.com) Inside this odd-looking building in Mallory Square (looking somewhat like a ship, somewhat like an old, rustic wrecker's shack) it is 1856, and shipwreck salvaging is the career of choice for many Key West citizens. The museum combines live actors and actual artifacts hauled up from the vessel Isaac Allerton, which sank in 1856 on the reef, and was found in 1985 by divers searching for the Atocha. Your tour guide is an actor in period clothes playing famed wrecker Asa Tift, and other actors portray crewmembers. Kids might enjoy this interactive museum more than, say, the Mel Fisher Maritime Museum, even though the Maritime has better artifacts. Climb the observation tower for a great view. Adults pay $10, $5 for kids.

KEY WEST MUSEUM OF ART & HISTORY IN THE CUSTOM HOUSE

(281 Front St. ☎ 305.295.6616

🖳 kwahs.com/customhouse.htm) Built in 1891, this Mallory Square building was at once the town's post office, courthouse, and center of government. A recent 9-million-dollar restoration reopened its doors as a "catch-all" museum and folk art gallery. Artwork by Mario Sanchez and Paul Collins coexist alongside memorabilia from Key West's salvaging days as the richest town in the U.S., then bankrupt, depression-era Key West. The museum also provides information on pirating and artifacts from Hemingway's life in the town. Some displays are interactive—others are just for viewing. Other exhibits change frequently, a recent crowd-pleaser being larger-than-life sculptures by J. Seward Johnson. Admission is $10 for adults, $5 for children. Audio tours are available.

KEY WEST SEA TURTLE MUSEUM

(200 Margaret St. ☎ 305.294.0209) Out on the docks behind the Turtle Kraals Restaurant, a tiny building, which once housed a turtle meat cannery is now devoted to the history of the industry and the conservation of sea turtles. Well-organized old photographs, shells, and skeletons document the bloody industry of turtling, when these animals were slaughtered in huge numbers for their meat. The end of the exhibit focuses on the current plight of sea turtles and conservation efforts. The curator is a colorful ex-ranger who knows plenty about Key West history and nature. Entrance is $3.

LIGHTHOUSE MUSEUM

(938 Whitehead St. ☎ 305.294.0012
🜚 kwahs.com/lighthouse.htm) Built in 1847, Key West's only lighthouse was erected far from water after a previous lighthouse toppled in a hurricane. The tower and nearby Keeper's Quarters have been restored and maintained as they were before the lighthouse was deactivated in 1969. The Keeper's Quarters displays maritime memorabilia and a history of the various keepers, plus a gift shop. Climb the 88-step, 90-foot tower for a fantastic view of the town. Adults pay $10, children cost $5.

MEL FISHER MARITIME MUSEUM

(200 Greene St. ☎ 305.294.2633 🜚 melfisher.org) One of Key West's most jealousy-inspiring moments occurred in 1985, when treasure hunter Mel Fisher found the "mother lode." The Atocha, the rear guard of a Spanish fleet of conquistadors, sank during a hurricane in 1622—loaded with gold, silver, jewels, and antiquities worth more than $400 million. Fisher spent 16 years and tens of thousands of dollars searching for the Atocha—and four lives were lost in the process. A prolonged legal battle ensued when the state of Florida tried to claim the treasure for themselves (and lost). You can view some of the booty and artifacts from the Atocha and its sister galleon, the Margarita, at the Maritime Museum. In 2010, two men managed to steal a gold bar from the museum worth $550,000. The whole thing was caught on a security camera, but so far, the culprits—and the treasure—are still at large. For a price, you can leave with a genuine artifact from the Atocha, sold in the gift shop. Admission is $7 for adults and $5 for kids.

OLDEST HOUSE MUSEUM

(322 Duval St. ☎ 305.294.9502 🖱 oirf.org/museums/oldest-house.htm) Built in 1829, the house was once the home of professional wrecker Francis Watlington and his wife and nine daughters. Back then, Key West was just a mosquito-ridden salt marsh—and the cure for yellow fever was mustard. The museum features original furnishings, ship models, maritime artifacts, items recovered from Keys waters, and a miniature 1850s-style dollhouse fashioned after the "conch" style houses of Key West and furnished in colonial and mid-Victorian styles. There is also an interactive map showing the locations of shipwrecks along the Keys. There is a lovely garden in back. Adults pay $5 to enter, $1 for children.

RIPLEY'S BELIEVE IT OR NOT! MUSEUM

(108 Duval St. ☎ 305.293.9939 🖱 ripleyskeywest.com) The Ripley's Believe it or Not! Museum adds to the circus-like atmosphere on the most "touristy" part of Duval Street. Surreal as it seems, one can view the skeleton of a giant prehistoric mastodon directly after stumbling out of the famous Hog's Breath Saloon. Ripley's quirky collection is at once a history lesson, a testament to the inventiveness of mankind, and an ode to circus freaks. Here, one can view handmade artifacts from indigenous tribes Ripley encountered throughout his travels, learn about the tallest man who ever lived, or gawk at a taxidermied two-headed rabbit. Ripley's is not recommended for young children or the squeamish, as some of the displays are rather unsettling. The $15 fee seems excessive, considering the whole collection can easily be viewed in under an hour.

SOUTHERNMOST HOUSE HISTORICAL MUSEUM

(1400 Duval St. ☎ 866.764.6633 🖱 southernmosthouse.com)
The house was built in 1896, and now serves as a guesthouse
with a museum on the first floor. The museum boasts a small,
strange mélange of artifacts, including 43 presidential signa-
tures (5 U.S. presidents have stayed at the house), letters from
Hemingway to his friends, and treasure from a shipwrecked
Spanish Galleon. $5 gets you through the doors, and also buys
you a complimentary drink by the pool. .

USS MOHAWK CGC MEMORIAL MUSEUM

(Memorial Park ☎ 305.292.5072) Take a self-guided $6 tour on
board a WW II warship. Built in 1934, this 165-foot ship was
involved in 14 attacks against Nazi Submarines on the Atlantic
Ocean, and was once stationed in Key West. There are plenty
of WWII artifacts on board.

WEST MARTELLO MUSEUM

(Atlantic Blvd. & White St. ☎ 305.294.3210) Built in 1862,
this old fort never saw battle, but was often used for target
practice by the Navy. Now, it hides one of the most beautiful
landscapes on the island. The grounds are maintained by the
Key West Garden Club. Giant banyan trees, palms, flowers,
and fruits trees stretch along winding walkways. At the top of
the hill, stop among the butterfly gardens to look out over the
deep blue ocean. Frequent art shows and native plant sales
draw crowds of locals. A $5 donation gets you through the
doors.

BIRDS AND WILDLIFE

When John James Audubon visited the Florida Keys in 1832, he was delighted by the variety of bird life he was able to document. Key West is still a birdwatcher's paradise, though development and human encroachment have taken their toll on the avian population. Still, many visitors come to the Keys to birdwatch and check rare specimens off their list such as the white crowned pigeon, great white heron, and the mangrove cuckoo. During migration, the island serves as a last stop for food and fresh water before vast expanses of ocean. Hundreds of species of waterfowl, songbirds, and raptors pass through Key West every year.

Eco-touring is the best way to see wildlife in the water. Out in the ocean, countless species of fish, crustaceans, marine mammals, and other sea creatures make their home and live out their dramas to the delight of observant snorkelers and scuba divers. Their continued existence depends on healthy offshore waters and a thriving barrier reef. Take the time to learn about the diversity of the Keys' marine life — you will be amazed.

Key West's native butterflies still decorate many a local garden, though pesticides have limited their numbers. Lizards are plentiful here: adorable geckos and anoles, and the prehistoric iguana. Iguanas are actually an "invasive species," meaning that at some point people bought them as pets then released them into the environment where they proliferated.

Luckily, there are a few places left in Key West where visitors can experience native wildlife. These spots, dedicated to preservation and education, shouldn't be missed. To quote what is perhaps the most quoted song in Key West: *"Don't it always seem to go that you don't know what you've got 'till it's gone. They paved paradise and put up a parking lot."*

KEY WEST GYPSY CHICKENS

Key West Gypsy chickens are the descendants of birds originally brought over from Cuba for cockfighting, egg-laying, and meat production. Unlike chickens bred for modern meat and egg production, Key West chickens are good flyers, great insect hunters, and are totally self-sufficient. Many tourists and locals enjoy sharing the island with these birds, and think they give Key West a laid back, Caribbean vibe.

Unfortunately, not all of Key West's residents appreciate being woken up by roosters crowing at all hours, or having their gardens scratched up by birds looking for scorpions. They complain about chicken poop, fret about the threat of "bird flu," and lobby the city commission to find a way to control— or eliminate—the local chicken population.

REEF RELIEF ENVIRONMENTAL CENTER

(631 Greene St. ☎ 305.294.3100 ♦ reefrelief.com) Reef Relief is a nonprofit organization that seeks to educate the public and raise money to support the Keys' ailing barrier reef. Its headquarters, located right next door to Conch Republic Seafood, offers multimedia educational displays, takeaway educational materials, and a quaint gift shop. It's free to come in and look around and friendly volunteers are available to answer questions. Donations are encouraged and will help support Reef Relief's noble effort.

DRY TORTUGAS NATIONAL PARK

(70 miles west of Key West, accessible by ferry) No serious birder or snorkeler should visit Key West without taking the ferry to the Dry Tortugas for a day. Out here are nesting sites for pelagic birds like the northern gannet, magnificent frigate-bird, brown booby, black noddy, and sooty tern just to name a few. The underwater-wildlife viewing is excellent too, as the water is pristine and full of corals.

ECO-DISCOVERY CENTER

(Truman Waterfront ☎ 305.292.0311) Before the entrance to Fort Zachary Taylor Historic Park sits the spanking new Eco-Discovery Center. The Center features interactive displays highlighting conservation efforts on land and in the ocean via the Florida Keys National Marine Sanctuary, two national parks, and four national wildlife refuges. Some exhibits feature live marine life. A high-definition theater screens a 17-minute video about Florida Keys National Marine Sanctuary by Bob Talbot. Visitors can watch coral spawning, learn about the armaments that once defended remote Fort Jefferson, or study the natural habitats of south Florida, from the Everglades to the coral reefs. Admission is free.

FORT ZACHARY TAYLOR STATE PARK ✪ Must See!

(Southard St. / Truman Annex) On the beach at "Fort Zach," wildlife-lovers can observe manificent frigates, black skimmers, and brown pelicans from shore, and great snorkling and the occasional sea turtle sighting in the water. Near the Fort itself is a nice series of nature trails where birders armed with cameras and binoculars are often seen stalking red-bellied woodpeckers and broad-winged hawks. In March of 2007, the

Loggerhead Kingbird, never before spotted in North America, showed up in the canopy, drawing birders from miles around.

KEY WEST AQUARIUM

(1 Whitehead St. ☎ 800.868.7482) This little Aquarium is actually Key West's oldest tourist attraction, opened in 1934. It's a great place to bring the kids, who will enjoy the touchtank full of starfish, sea cucumbers, and horseshoe crabs. Pools filled with sea turtles, stingrays, and nurse sharks are great for viewing. Giant moray eels, goliath grouper, and enormous spiny lobster are highlights — and during the narrated tour, the tour guide lets everyone touch a shark! This small and intimate aquarium is perfect for children and can be viewed at a leisurely pace within an hour. Admission is $12 for adults, $5 for children.

KEY WEST BUTTERFLY & NATURE CONSERVATORY

(1316 Duval St. ☎ 305.296.2988) At the conservatory, you will experience one of the most tranquil, visually pleasing hours you can spend on the island. First, you enter a small room with a video screen showing the life span of a butterfly. Displays of caterpillars and other assorted lizards and frogs, maps, and other information prepare you for what you will see inside the conservatory. Then, you pass through two sets of doors into a scene that will surely take your breath away. Among flowering, lush plants, alongside a tranquil, bubbling streams, while gentle music plays, you will behold hundreds and hundreds of butterflies. They are big and small, of every imaginable color and pattern. There are also brightly colored songbirds and beautiful golden koi, turtles, and quail to delight your eyes. Everyone moves slowly in here (lest you step on one of the marvelous creatures). You can sit on a bench and watch the butterflies flutter around you, or walk the path and find something new around every turn. Either way, you will feel your tension disappear into the humid air. There is a gift shop with lots of dainty things for sale.

KEY WEST NATURE PRESERVE

(Atlantic Ave.) Along the bike trail on Atlantic Avenue, between two condominium complexes, signs mark two entrances to a tiny, city-owned wetland preserve. Two small trails lead through through wetlands to a secluded strip of beach, where many wading birds take advantage of beachfront property void of sunbathing, splashing humans. This tiny, neglected preserve is the best spot on the island to observe Cardisoma guanhumi, also known as the giant crab or the blue land crab.

KEY WEST NATIONAL WILDLIFE REFUGE

(☎ 305.872.3329) Immediately west of the island and accessible only by boat, the Key West National Wildlife Refuge was established in 1908 by President Roosevelt as a preserve and breeding ground for native birds and other wildlife. This refuge was the first established in the Florida Keys and one of the earliest refuges in the United States. The refuge encompasses more than 200,000 acres with 2,000 acres of land, and is home to more than 250 species of birds and is important for sea turtle nesting. The islands are predominately mangrove with a few beaches and salt ponds. It is managed as a satellite of the National Key Deer Refuge on Big Pine Key. Two of the Key West NWR islands have portions of their beaches closed to the public for the sensitive habitat they contain. The remainder of the beaches, including those at the Marquesas Keys, is open during daylight hours for compatible, wildlife-oriented recreational uses such as wildlife observation, nature photography and environmental education. Camping is not allowed on refuge lands.

KEY WEST TROPICAL FOREST AND BOTANICAL GARDENS

(5210 College Rd, Stock Island) The garden has three freshwater ponds, one that is visible from the sky, attracting birds as they pass through for migration. The plants are well-labeled and the park is home to plenty of butterflies, lizards and other critters to observe.

LITTLE HAMACA PARK

(Government Rd) Little Hamaca Park is far off the beaten path in New Town and a bit hard to find. Look for the sign on Flagler pointing toward Government Road. Drive slowly along the winding road past saltponds small plane parking and runways. There is an entrance to a walking trail on the left (or continue driving through an abandoned police training area to a paintball field among a salt pond restoration project.) Owned by the Department of the Interior, Little Hamaca Park is the only place in Key West where you can see what the island used to look like before the condos and strip malls and tacky tee shirt shops. The park boasts ten acres with a half-mile-long trail through four unique ecosystems: a mangrove swamp, a salt marsh, a buttonwood wetland and a hardwood hammock, ending at the Riviera Canal. Sometimes, you can walk the whole trail without seeing another human being — but be wary about going after dark, when, rumor has it, the park becomes a gay cruising spot. Signs along the path educate you on each habitat. Within the park, you may spot anything from nesting peregrine falcons to flocks of white-crowned pigeons.

NANCY FORESTER'S SECRET GARDEN

(1 Freeschool Ln. ☎ 305.294.0015) Ms. Forester's breathtaking one-acre garden is like stepping into a different word where everything is calm and luminous. A rainforest-like canopy envelops you as you walk winding mulch trails. Flowering orchids, gorgeous mosses, and rare tropical plants from around the world greet you at every turn. Some of the plants you can see here are actually endangered or extinct in their natural environment. Lazy cats and cages with parrots and cockatoos rescued from abuse or neglect situations add to the ambiance. There is a small art gallery on site with a botanical theme worth wandering into. Admission is a mere $6—and donations are greatly appreciated. To find the garden, head down Simonton and look for the Heron House. Freeschool Lane is across the street.

RIGGS WILDLIFE REFUGE & BRIDLE PATH

(South Roosevelt Blvd.) If you happen to be spending the day at Smather's Beach, walk to the end of the beach near to the airport, cross over to the other side of the road and peek into the salt ponds. The ponds serve as a nursery for many species of fish and birds. Ospreys are common here, as are many species of wading birds that feed on tiny fish and crustaceans. A bike path winds along the outskirts of the ponds, but trees block the view of the ponds for the most part.

SHERIFF'S ZOO

(5501 College Rd., Stock Island) If you happen to be in Key West on the 2nd or 4th Sunday of each month and feel like doing something away from downtown Key West, a small zoo opens beneath the jail on Stock island from 1 to 3 p.m. That's right—a zoo under the jail. Here, you will see rescued farm animals like donkeys, goats and pigs, and exotic pets like ferrets, tortoises, sloths, rabbits and even a Key deer! You can pet some of the animals. Admission is free, donations are appreciated.

SONNY MCCOY INDIGENOUS PARK / KEY WEST WILDLIFE CENTER

(1801 White St. ☎ 305.292.1008 ♻ keywestwildlifecenter.org) Along the cement pathway of the Indigenous Park, you will see only plants that are native to Key West soil, some of which are labeled. The park is a designated wildlife refuge (owned by the Department of the Interior) and bird watching here is excellent. Commonly seen are broad wing and cooper's hawks, American kestrels, anhingas, white crowned pigeons, purple gallinules, scarlet tanagers, and belted kingfishers. At the end of the park, a freshwater pond—courtesy of the Audubon Society—is watering hole to birds, turtles, iguanas, tree frogs, dragonflies, and butterflies. Within the park the Key West Wildife Center rescues and rehabilitates injured wildlife. A large aviary displays wild birds whose injuries prevent their return to the wild, such as Ozzie the osprey who lost a wing, Bonnie the broadwing hawk who lost an eye, or Hoppy, the one-legged laughing gull. Though admission to the park is free, the Wildlife Center counts on donations to fund its rescue operations, medications, vet care, feeding, and housing of their animals, so give generously. Birdwatchers: before you leave, head across White St. and check out the **Monroe County Bird Sanctuary:** a little pond surrounded by trees in the park on the corner of White Street and Casa Marina Court. It's a popular warbler and wading bird hang-out.

OTHER LANDMARK SIGHTS

A few other places in Key West stand out for tourists. If your tour or plans don't already take you to one of these places, you will probably want to find a way—if even as a short excursion—to see them.

THE "SOUTHERNMOST POINT"

(Whitehead and South Street) There really is a "southernmost point" in the continental U.S. (not counting Hawaii, which is about 400 miles further south). Located just off the beaten path, there is a marker, shaped like an odd bouy, which you can walk right up to. The marker reads "The Conch Republic – 90 Miles to Cuba – Southernmost Point – Continental U.S.A. – Key West, FL – Home of the Sunset." The only thing to do here is get a souvenir photo standing next to the bouy, and you will usually have to stand in line to do so.

MALLORY SQUARE ✪ Must See!

Mallory Square, especially at sunset, is where many of Key West tourists—and locals, as well—make their way as the night begins. This is the home of the famous "Sunset Celebration," where onlookers watch the sunset. This area, at the north end of Duval Street, is also near where the cruise ships dock and where most of the Duval Street hubbub is. So expect crowds. Lots of crowds. But you can't avoid it.

The "celebration" is a daily ritual. It is, perhaps, the quintessential Key West experience in all its gaudy, carnival-like glory—an absolute must-see for visitors. The premise is simple: watch the sunset in one of the most spectacular, unobstructed views ever. Plus, local merchants and street performers gather as tourists ad-mire Nature's show.

In the sixties, back when Key West was a haven for writers, artists, and ne'er-do-wells, people began gathering at the edge of the Gulf of Mexico to drink, smoke, and beat drums as the sun went down. Nowadays, it is a little more complicated, and artists and hawkers must apply via lottery for a choice spot on the pier. The sunset is still spectacular, but getting a photo of it without some tourists' heads in it is darned near impossible. If you don't like crowds, try going on a weekday off-season. What you will see: local arts and crafts for sale. Fire dancers. Jugglers. Sword swallowers. Musicians. A guy endangering all nine lives of his cats by making them jump through flaming hoops. Escape artists.

Beaches and Water Sports

Chances are, since you're already in Key West, you'll want to spend some time out on the water or under the famous Florida sun—in some of the country's most beautiful waterscapes.

PUBLIC BEACHES

Key West has several public beaches, most of them on the South side of the island. They are a great place to kick back and relax, take a romantic stroll, or spend the day with friends or family. Kids love playing in our shallow, calm waters—and people of all ages enjoy that the ocean is warm year-round. Key West's beaches have a character all their own. The soft white sand is actually imported from the Bahamas: underneath is pure rock and dead coral. Unfortunately, the imported sand falls into the ocean where it smothers and kills the seagrass. The dead seagrass washes ashore, often causing the beaches to have a distinctly rotten egg smell. The water is blue and green and every shade in between. Often, it is perfectly still and clear.

Before heading out, you'll want to check for beach advisories before you pack up and head to the water. Look for signs posted on the beach advising against swimming. Also, the local newspapers will mention if a beach has recently tested positive for contamination. You can check the results online (● *http://esetappsdoh. doh.state.fl.us/irm00beachwater/*).

DOG BEACH

(Waddell St.) As per its name, locals frequently bring their dogs to this tiny beach and let them splash through the ocean to their doggy hearts' content. This is actually a nice spot for swimming, too—the water is deeper than most Key West beaches, and the floor is sandy rather than seagrassy. Tropical fish congregate under the nearby pier, and they often come investigate swimmers. Dog Beach is next to an excellent upscale restaurant, Louie's Backyard (open for lunch and dinner). Maybe you'll find one of the unopened, top-shelf bottles of liquor that washed out to the sea when the restaurant was clobbered by Hurricane Wilma. Dog beach is never tested for contamination, but its proximity to frequently-tested South Beach means you can probably trust those results to be the same.

HIGGS BEACH

(Atlantic Ave.) Higgs has volleyball nets, barbeque pits, and picnic table pavilions. There is a decent Italian bistro called Salute right on the beach, and there are public bathrooms. Nearby, the White Street Pier offers great fishing and a gorgeous walk out on the sea. The water here is very shallow. Unfortunately, Higgs is probably the beach most often issued swimming advisories. Also, the local homeless population has taken up residence on most of the picnic tables.

REST BEACH

(Atlantic Ave.) Right next to Higgs, narrow Rest Beach offers access to the White Street Pier and some picnic tables surrounded by beautiful landscaping. If water has tested poorly at Higgs, you should avoid Rest Beach as well.

SIMONTON BEACH

(Simonton St) This is the only public beach on the island that overlooks the Gulf of Mexico instead of the Atlantic Ocean. It is the size of a small room, and has public bathrooms. There are often several homeless camped out here, but the water is deep enough for a decent swim and the floor is nice and sandy.

SMATHERS BEACH

(S. Roosevelt Blvd.) Smathers is the longest beach on the island, and the prettiest for sunbathing. Weddings are often held here, and it is party central during spring break. It has volleyball nets, picnic tables, bathrooms, cold showers, kayak and rubber raft rentals, and several motorstands offering hotdogs, hamburgers, and ice cream. Unfortunately, the swimming here isn't great: the water is shallow and the ocean floor is slimy with seagrass. The best way to enjoy the water is to rent or buy a rubber raft—then jump on and float. There is little chance of a rough tide pulling you out to sea.

SOUTH BEACH

(Duval St.) This little beach is maintained by Southermost Beach Cafe—a charming open-air bistro right on the beach. Grab a piña colada and a lounge chair. This beach is swimmable, but check recent swimming advisories first. It's one of the more frequently contaminated beaches on the island.

FORT ZACHARY TAYLOR ✪ Must See!

(Southard St.) This is by far the nicest beach in Key West, and the beach least often testing positive for contamination. It's also the only public beach in Key West that charges admission. The water at Fort Zach is deep, clear and cool, excellent for swimming. There's good snorkeling near the rocks, and an entire section of the beach is devoted to fishing. Fort Zach also offers kayak and snorkel gear rentals, and has bathrooms and cold showers. You can grab a slice of pizza and a beer at the snack shack, then rest at a picnic table under towering Australian Pines.

GETTING OUT ON THE WATER

Some visitors come just to party on Duval Street. The rest come here for the ocean. Tranquil, warm, and blue, the offshore waters of Key West have everything to offer. 3 miles out is the only barrier reef in North America. Go see it while you can—the experts agree that the reef is in trouble. We can blame a combination of pollution, global warming and offshore drilling in the Gulf of Mexico. The reef is home to thousands of fish, crustaceans, anemones, and other fascinating creatures. There are sea turtles, dolphins and manatee in our waters, and hundreds of people come out every year just to encounter them.

Diving, snorkeling, and fishing are great around the reef. Closer to shore, you can try kayaking, jet-skiing or parasailing. A romantic sunset cruise with wine might be just the thing. These are just some of the water activities available in Key West. Take a walk through the docks behind the restaurants at the Historic Seaport, or behind the Westin Resort near Mallory Square. The boat captains put up signs and put out brochures so you can see what each boat has to offer.

Equipment and instruction are always included for your activity: snorkel trips include snorkel gear and floatation devices, fishing trips include bait, reels, and a temporary saltwater fishing license, and scuba trips come fully equipped. Refreshments of some sort are almost always offered, and yes, there are bathrooms on board. The boat's staff is invariably knowledgeable and concerned for your safety and enjoyment. You will never meet people who love their jobs more than the captains and crews of Key West's charter boats!

"Party boats" are an affordable way to enjoy the water for a few hours, but you will share the trip with 30 or more other people. Smaller boats offer more intimate and expensive trips with groups of 6 to 12. If money is no object, you or your group can even rent a boat with a captain who will customize your day.

When you're out on the water, pleae be careful of our fragile environment. Choose a biodegradable sunscreen, do not throw anything overboard, and do not take home shells or bits of living or dead coral as "souvenirs". Be careful not to step, touch or anchor upon the reef. Coral is made up of living organisms that are easily damaged by contact. With a little caution, we can make sure Key West's waters will be enjoyable for generations to come.

ECO-TOURING

Eco-touring allows us to enjoy the ocean without causing it damage. The following charters take pride in revealing the natural wonders of the sea in an eco-friendly manner. They are all about education and conservation. Whether you want to see dolphins, sharks, birds or sea turtles, these guides know the best spots and can tell you all about the animals you are seeing.

AQUA CHARTERS

(Garrison Bight ☎ 305.304.4392 ⬤ aquacharters.com) Captain Katey Quinn will take your party aboard a 23-foot Chris Craft snorkeling, dolphin watching, eco-touring the "back country," or just on a sunset cruise. A three-hour dolphin watch is $85 per person (3 hours, 2 person minimum) while sunset cruises with champagne run at $225. Half-day charters and private snorkel trips are $350.

BLUE PLANET KAYAK

(☎ 212.209.3370 ⬤ blue-planet-kayak.com) Guides with backgrounds in marine biology will reveal the mysteries of nature in an intimate kayak tour which highlights conservation of and consideration for wildlife. Explore Boca Chica's tidal creeks or skirt a mangrove rookery in the back country. Or, take a moonlight tour and see what comes out at night. Pricing is determined by the distance paddled.

DANGER CHARTERS

(Westin Marina ☎ 305.296.3272 ⬤ dangercharters.com) Captain Wayne Fox takes passengers off the beaten path on board an American sailing craft or a sleek schooner. Visit the Key West National Wildlife Refuge, where you will set anchor and kayak through the mangroves. Snorkel in a secluded patch reef. It costs around $75 for a half-day, or $90 for a full day. Danger's Wind and Wine Sunset Cruise offers wine tasting and hors d'oeuvres for $65.

DOLPHIN WATCH

(Historic Seaport ☎ 305.294.6306 ⬤ dolphinwatch.org) Captain Ron Cranning has been watching the same group of local bottlenose dolphins since 1986, and he knows these creatures individually. Geared toward education and conservation, this 31-foot Gemini catamaran with comfy interior offers four hours of dolphin-watching and snorkeling for $85 per person (6 person maximum) or opt for a half day $500 private charter.

KEY WEST EXTREME ADVENTURES SHARK TOURS
(Westin Marina ☎ 305.508.1951 ☗ kwextremeadventures.com)
Local wildlife experts Captain Ken Harris and Captain Dave Harris conduct three and a half hour tours aboard a a 34-foot catamaran. The "Tiger Cat" was designed to preserve the ecology of backcountry waters utilizing a power-pole system in lieu of anchors, eliminating potential damage to the sea grass and coral bottom. You will get to see the apex predators of the oceans up close, as well as turtles, sting rays, and other wildlife.

SUNNY DAY'S ISLAND EXPRESS
(Historic Seaport ☎ 305.293.5144 ☗ sunnydayskeywest.com)
Looe Key is as a national marine sanctuary with a very large coral reef system that measures 200 yards wide and 800 yards across. The area has an impressive variety of depths, making snorkeling or scuba diving at different locations in the same area highly diverse. This is the only boat that travels to Looe Key from Key West (there are others in Big Pine) Adult fare is $ 85, Children $ 50, and an all-you-can-eat buffet lunch is included.

WILD DOLPHIN ADVENTURES

(Historic Seaport ☎ 305.296.3737

📱 wilddolphinadventures.com) This eco-tour travels to where dolphins play aboard the 28-foot "Coral Reefer." Snorkel in the reef or just lounge on deck. They offer two 3-hour trips per day costing $85 per person. Private, customized charters are also available. There is a maximum six passengers.

SNORKELING, DIVING AND SNUBA

The waters off Key West offer excellent opportunites for diving, snorkeling and snuba. Many boats take visitors to see the Keys' barrier reef--the only one in North America. The most popular reefs for snorkeling and diving are the areas known as Sand Key, the Dry Rocks and Cotrell Reef.

A number of artificial reefs, "wrecks" stripped of pollutants and sank intentionally, also attract underwater enthusiasts. "Alexander's Wreck," a.k.a. the USS Amesbury, is a wreck in two peices which is in water shallow enough for snorkeling. Joe's Tug is a shimp boat which was supposed to sink in Miami but was hijaked by locals. Cayman Salvage is a 1930's Coast Guard Ship. The newest and largest wreck is the Gen. Hoyt S. Vandenberg, affectionately nicknamed "the Vandy" by locals. This 522 foot Navy transport ship sank in 2009.

BLUE ICE SAILING

(Historic Seaport ☎ 305.294.5856 📱 blueicesailing.com) "Blue Ice" is a 47-foot, 6-passenger Sloop. Sail and snorkel for a full day or half ($700 or $450), enjoy a two-hour sunset cruise

Key West Lighthouse (© *iStockphoto.com/ travelif*)

The Overseas Highway *(© iStockphoto.com/Pgiam)*

Key West Residential Street *(© iStockphoto.com/Cristian Lazzari)*

Palm Tree (© *iStockphoto.com/Steven Gibson*)

($290.) They also do weddings. Captain and crew, beverages, beer, wine, champagne, and snacks are included.

LOST REEF ADVENTURES
(**Historic Seaport** ☎ **305.296.9737**) Dive the artificial reefs in the waters of Key West, including "Joe's Tug," "Cayman Salvage," and the Vandenberg, or check out natural sites like Sambo Reef. Trips cost about $45 to snorkel and $105 to dive, with everything you need included. Both morning and afternoon trips are available.

SEA EAGLE
(**Historic Seaport** ☎ **305.296.8865** 🖥 **captainscorner.com**) Feel like James Bond for a day riding the 60-foot dive vessel featured in *License to Kill*. Get your training at Captain's Corner Dive Center, and then join one of two dive/snorkel trips per day. It's $35 to snorkel, $40 to dive. They also offer exclusive trips to the sites of the Spanish treasure ship, the Atocha and the English merchant-slaver, the Henrietta Marie.

SNUBA OF KEY WEST
(**Garrison Bight** ☎ **305.292.4616** 🖥 **snubakeywest.com**) Float below the surface of the water without scuba certification or cumbersome breathing apparatus. The "Miss Sunshine" is a 33-foot catamaran, which carries 12. Three trips depart daily at a cost of $99 per person. Kids pay $79, and anyone just along for the ride pays $44. All equipment and instruction is provided.

SUBTROPIC DIVE CENTER

(Garrison Bight ☎ 305.296.9914 ⬤ subtropic.com) Visit two wrecks, two reef sites, or one wreck and one reef site for $95 (full equipment provided). Bring the family—those not certified to scuba can snorkel for $40 or sunbathe for $25. Two trips are made daily, and night dives are also offered. Both of their Burpees are also available for private charters.

VENUS CHARTERS

(Garrison Bight ☎ 305.292.9403 ⬤ venuscharters.com) Captains Karen and Debra offer women-only snorkeling and dolphin watching, or light tackle fishing cruises, as well as private charters that are open to all. Venus is a 25-foot Proline open fisherman. Charters are for 2 to 6 passengers, three hours for $85 per person. Commitment ceremony cruises cost upwards of $300.

FISHING

Many people feel that fishing is a great way to feel connected to the ocean—and nothing tastes quite so good as fresh fish you caught yourself! The Marquesas, 30 miles from Key West, offer flats sportsfishing for snook, bonefish and tarpon. Near the reef, yellowtail snapper, mahi-mahi, hogfish and grouper are popular catch-and-eat fish. But please do not take more than you will eat, practice responsible catchand-release ethics, and follow laws as to size minimums and catch quotas. Also, be sure to properly discard monofilament. Remember: fishhooks and fishing line pose extreme dangers to wildlife.

Of course, certain fish are protected and off limits to anglers. The most notable of these fish are Goliath groupers, a.k.a "jewfish." Goliaths were once abundant in the Keys. These huge groupers are slow to mature, have no fear of humans, and are famous for curiously swimming up to divers, even if the divers carries a spear gun. By the early nineties the species was nearly wiped out by fishing, the government stepped in and declared them a protected species.

GULF STREAM III
(Amberjk Pr 8, City Marina ☎ 305.296.8494
● keywestpartyboat.com) Family fishing for grouper, snapper, and yellowtail is what you'll get aboard this 65' foot party boat. Free bait, license, and tackle come with a $3 rod rental. Seven hours of fishing costs $50, day or night. Sunbathers pay half price.

KEY WEST FISHING CHARTERS
(☎ 305.304.0154 ● bonefishingkeywest.com) For about $150 a day, Captain Lenny takes anglers to the Marquesas, a group of uninhabited islands about 30 miles from Key West which are protected as part of the Key West National Wildlife Refuge. The Marquesas form a calm atoll, where fishing in the flats for bonefish, tarpon and permit are legendary.

TORTUGA IV
(Conch Harbor ☎ 305.293.1189 ● tortugacharters.com) Fish for amberjack, snapper, yellowtail, grouper, cobia, mackerel, and Key West grunts aboard a 62-foot catamaran hull. Rods, bait, and fishing license are provided, as are snacks, sandwiches, beverages, plus a sundeck for non-fishers. The boat takes up

to 49 passengers, and trips last about four hours. Prices range from $45 - $150 and above.

CRUISING

For a quick jaunt out to the water, nothing beats a sunset cruise with complimentary drinks.

SCHOONER LIBERTY CLIPPER CRUISES
(Westin Marina, Historic Seaport ☎ 305.292.0332
📱 libertyfleet.com) Take a two-hour sail morning or afternoon for $45 and under, or the sunset cruise for $57 (adults) and $35 (kids) Enjoy complimentary beer, wine, champagne, and soda aboard the 80-foot Schooner Liberty or the 125-foot Schooner Liberty Clipper. Dinner sails feature a Caribbean barbeque dinner.

SUNSET WATERSPORTS
(Historic Seaport ☎ 305.296.2554 📱 sunsetwatersports.info)
View Key West's famous sunset on this 2-hour sunset cruise with Island music, free draft beer and soft drinks, all for $20. Sunset also offers parasailing for $29-$39, and a snorkel safari tour through the marine sanctuary for $69. Sunset even lets you do it all for $99—including Wave Runners, windsurfing, snorkeling, and kayaking—with a free BBQ lunch.

CLOTHING OPTIONAL

Get back to nature while you're… getting back to nature!

BLU Q

(Historic Seaport ☎ 305.923.7245 🖱 captainstevekw.com)
Captain Steve presents all-gay, clothing-optional sailing, snorkeling, and kayaking, and sunset cruising on a catamaran. Half-day trips are $75 per person, shorter sunset cruises are $35.

SKINNY DIPPER CRUISES

(Garrison Bight ☎ 305.240.0517 🖱 skinnydippercruises.com)
Timothy Brown captains this 28-foot cruiser yacht that specializes in intimate (4-6 people) clothing optional gay cruises, reef and wreck snorkel trips, and daily sunset cruises—as you wish. There is a full bar and snacks, shower, and beds. Captain Brown is an ordained minister, and will marry or perform a union. The cost is $125 per person for three hours, and $75 for the daily sunset cruise.

YOU BE THE CAPTAIN

These charters allow you to have some say in your itinerary. Get a captain and crew, or, (if you are a licensed captain) drive yourself.

FLORIDA KEYS BOAT RENTALS

(☎ 305.664.2203 🖱 keysboat.com) Rent anything from an 8-foot paddleboat to a 30-foot Sea-Ray, by the hour, day, or weekly. They also offer fishing excursions. They can set you up with a captain at your request, or simply stock your boat with snorkel or fishing gear.

KEY WEST BOAT AND BREAKFAST CHARTERS
(Historic Seaport ☎ 305.295.2631

📱 keywestsailingadventure.com) Live aboard a yacht. Stay a weekend or a week. For every three days you stay with them, they include a half day sail to the reef with lunch and snorkel gear on board. Pricing starts at $295.00 for two persons, per night. This includes a half-day reef sail. They also charter yachts for weddings, snorkel trips, or sunset cruises.

OTHER WATER ADVENTURES

There are all kinds of charter boats and water adventure possibilities "floating" around Key West. Following are a few of the unique experiences that go a bit beyond the basics.

DRY TORTUGAS FERRY
(Historic Seaport ☎ 305.294.7009 📱 yankeefreedom.com) 70 miles West of Key West, on one of several tiny islands sits Dry Tortugas National Park. Reasons to visit include Historic Fort Jefferson, a beautiful beach, amazing snorkeling, and prolific bird life. The best way to get there is on board the Yankee Freedom II—a high-speed catamaran. They offer breakfast and lunch, professional tour guides at sea and at the park, and complimentary snorkeling equipment. An entertainment system plays throughout the trip. A picnic buffet is provided on the island. The ferry departs daily at 8 a.m., and returns at 5:30 p.m. Adults cost $129, kids $89. Tent campers on the park get a discount.

FURY WATER ADVENTURES

(Historic Seaport ☎ 305.294.8899 ▯ furykeywest.com) Fury offers reef snorkeling, jet skiing, parasailing, and kayaking aboard a catamaran. Or, combine them all for a full-day "Ultimate Adventure" ending in a sunset sail. They also offer a 90-minute tour in a glass-bottom boat, plus a variety of combo packages. Snorkeling trips are in the high $30-range for a three-hour tour, half that for kids. Parasailing is $40 for an hour, and the glass-bottom boat is $35 for adults, $15 for children. The sunset sail with live music is $49 per person, lasting two hours. Teenagers will enjoy Fury's Ultimate Adventure, conisiting of a half day of Fury's ocean water park featuring jet skiing, kayaking, parasailing, rock climbing, and a water trampoline plus a picnic dinner. The Fury's Gay & Lesbian Ultimate Adventure offers the same, but with a DJ, unlimited beer, wine, and champagne.

GLASSBOTTOM BOAT DISCOVERY

(Historic Seaport ☎ 305.293.0099

▯ **discoveryunderseatours.com)** See the action of the coral reef while keeping perfectly dry. The whole family will enjoy the viewing room—20 large windows set in the sides of the hull of the Discovery at a 45-degree angle. The tour is fully narrated by our knowledgeable crew on board this 78-foot vessel. Up top is a spacious sundeck with a snack bar offering soda, beer, wine and snacks. The boat goes out three times daily—the evening cruise offers complimentary champagne. Cost is $35 for adults, $16 for kids (children under 4 ride free).

SKI KEY WEST

(Galleon Marina ☎ 305.292.2210 🖱 skikeywest.com) Rent a Wave Runner by the hour and explore on your own, or join a tour that takes you 26 miles around Key West. You will visit a submarine pit built by the Navy in World War II, the "Southernmost Point", secluded islands, shipwrecks, mangroves, and a dolphin playground. Travelers must be 22 years of age to operate wave runner alone. Guided tours are $130, or pay $110 per hour.

SUNNY DAYS CATAMARANS

(Historic Seaport ☎ 305.293.5144

🖱 **sunnydayskeywest.com)** Sunny Days offers reef snorkel trips aboard the "Reef Express" or the "Caribbean Spirit." Ride for 3 hours with two stops --for $35 adult, $22 kids. They also offer $30 sunset cruises and $45 dolphin watches. "Fast Cat II" makes a daily trip to Dry Tortugas for $120, $85 for children.

Retail Key West

There is plenty of shopping in Key West. Like any cruise ship port, downtown Duval Street hosts an array of expensive jewelry stores, overpriced boutiques, tacky curio shops, and ubiquitous chains like Banana Republic and Coach. Luckily, there are a few places in Key West that offer a unique experience when it comes to retail.

BESAME MUCHO

(315 Petronia St. ☎ 305.294.1928 📱 besamemucho.net) This lovely little gift shop was established in 1999 in the heart of Bahama Village. Besame Mucho features housewares, bath products, clothing, jewelry, gifts, art, etc. with a distinctly Old-World Cuban vibe. You will smell the perfume from Besame Mucho from the street. Inside, all is elegant, languid, and tropical. The store features products from Santa Maria Novella, Kiehl's, and Dr. Hauschka, to name a few.

BLOND GIRAFFE

(2 Locations: 107 Simonton St. ☎ 305.296.9174 & 802 Duval St. ☎ 305.293.7874 📱 blondgiraffe.com) This Key West and Miami chain features what is said to be the best Key Lime Pie anywhere. They also feature other sweets and souvenirs. There is really not much seating at the Blond Giraffe—you're supposed to get your goodies to go, or take them home with you. You can even order pies online and they will ship them to you. You can watch the pies being made at the "Factory" on Simonton Street. Be warned that service at this location is often lackadaisical.

BLUE

(718 Caroline St. ☎ 305.292.5172 🖱 blueislandstore.com) Step away from the painfully trendy, midriff-baring shirts and faux-cowboy hats of the boutiques on Duval Street. Blue features "haute-casual," comfortable, sophisticated, and feminine clothing with tropical accents. Besides clothing and accessories, they feature the jewelry of local artist David Symons. The staff is lovely and helpful. There is also a Blue in Islamorada.

CONCH REPUBLIC CIGAR FACTORY

(512 Greene St. ☎ 305.295.9036 🖱 conch-cigars.com) Cigar-making used to be a major industry in Key West. This shop hearkens back to that time with an excellent selection of imported and locally rolled smokes, including the famous El Hemingway. Of course, buying or selling Cuban-made cigars is illegal, so the "Cuban cigars" you see here are domestic cigars made from tobacco grown from seeds that were brought from Cuba decades ago. They also feature cigars from Dominica and Honduras.

FAIRVILLA MEGASTORE

(520 Front St. ☎ 305.292.0448 🖱 fairvilla.com) Fairvilla celebrates everything erotic. The store features adult costumes, make-up, lubes, films, and all sorts of sexy, naughty fun "toys". Fairvilla is for adults only, and is packed to the gills in the days nearing Fantasy Fest. You'll marvel at the huge selections of everything and everything your dirty heart desires. The store is clean and the staff is very open-minded and helpful.

FASTBUCK FREDDIE'S ✪ Must See!

(500 Duval St. ☎ 305.294.2007 📱 fastbuckfreddies.com)
You can't miss this huge department store in a central location on Duval with often-changing, zany window displays. Fastbuck's features a mish-mosh of clothes, housewares, gifts, and furniture, all chosen with whimsical flair. Merchandise is from around the world, and many pieces are one of a kind or designed and built just for Fastbuck Freddie's. Items are artfully displayed, and just walking around in this store is a good time. This is not a discount outlet—prices are high, and the store is often a "zoo", especially around the holidays. But Fastbuck's festive atmosphere and fun merchandise have made it a favorite since opening in 1976.

HALF-BUCK FREDDIE'S

(726 Caroline St. ☎ 305.294.6799) This small, discount outlet is the little sister to Fastbuck Freddie's and features out-of-season, slightly damaged or discarded bargains from the main store. There is some great quirky merchandise here, and the prices are more reasonable than the main store. You have to really dig in and look for what you want—or just see what catches your eye. Locals love Half-Buck, as do thrifty tourists.

KERMIT'S KEY LIME SHOPPE

(200 Elizabeth St. ☎ 305.296.0806 📱 keylimeshop.com) The Key Lime Shoppe celebrates the famous fruit through pies, candies, sauces, soaps, shampoos… the list goes on. The owner, Kermit, is a character often standing out front of his store dressed in chef white's and his signature huge chef's hat waving to passer-bys. His Key Lime Pie is very good, and has even been featured on the Food Network. The store is on a fun corner in the Waterfront district, surrounded by shops, galleries, and bars.

KEY WEST TOY FACTORY

(291 Front St. ☎ 305.296.0003) Upstairs in Clinton Square Market, the Toy Factory sells quality toys. Kids will love their magic section and "Imagineering Workshop." They can even ride a carousel, partake in arts and craft, enjoy a free magic show, or visit with the owner's pet kinkajou, Izzy. The Toy Factory encourages kids (and their parents) to stay and play.

KINO SANDALS

(107 Fitzpatrick St. ☎ 305.294.5044 ☗ kinosandalfactory.com) Watch your sandals being made! All of the sandals sold at Kino Sandals are handmade using natural leather uppers and natural rubber soles. They are assembled and glued by hand using a traditional Cuban method. These affordable, comfortable, durable, and nice-looking sandals have been made in this same manner since the company's founder came from Cuba to Key West in the 1960s.

PEPPERS OF KEY WEST

(603 Greene St. ☎ 305.295.9333 ☗ peppersofkeywest.com) If you like hot sauce, you will love Peppers. They have an astounding variety of hot sauce, barbeque sauce, salsa, seasonings, etc., many with Key West-inspired flavors and zany names (for example, "Iguana Gold Island Pepper Sauce" or "Fighting Cock Kentucky Bourbon BBQ Sauce"). There is often plenty of free sampling involved when you visit the store. The owners and staff are really into their spices and will gladly direct you toward exactly what your tastebuds are looking for.

Dining and Drinking

———●✪

Key West has a big culinary scene for such a tiny island. Though it's not as cosmopolitan as Miami or even Coral Gables on the mainland, there's some darned good restaurants here, and a lot of them. Restaurants are big business here, and everyone, local or tourist, will gladly recommend their personal favorite if asked. The Keys' "Floribbean" cuisine is a mixture of influences from the Southern U.S., Cuba, and the Bahamas. Key West also has restaurants in the downtown area representing Japan, China, Thailand, Italy, France, Germany, Cuba, Columbia and Mexico. Though no produce is grown commercially on the island (not even the infamous Key Lime) farmlands abound in Homestead just on the mainland. Citrus and tomatoes are major crops in Homestead, as are avocados and, strangely, lychee.

Seafood is fresh and abundant throughout the Keys. Grouper, mahi-mahi (also called dolphin) and yellowtail snapper are most often locally caught. Cobia, wahoo, and tuna are not uncommon. Queen Conch was once a staple of the regional cuisine, but these days it is imported from the Bahamas—it is illegal to harvest the endangered Queen Conch in the Florida Keys. Spiny lobster is a local delicacy, different from its cold-water counterparts in that is lacks claws and the tail meat is gamier. Almost every restaurant serves their version of Key Lime Pie—traditionally with graham cracker crust, but sometimes with chocolate or regular piecrust.

Prices are hefty in Key West, as in any tourist town, so don't go into shock when the waiter hands you your check. Tipping is expected, generally around 20% - Key West is an expensive town to live in on a waiter's salary. Dress in Key West is always casual—but don't expect to get away with dining in your bathing suit or barefoot.

We will not dwell on chain restaurants like Wendy's and Denny's, though they all exist downtown. We've also left out some of the restaurants at the big hotels, which are not locally owned.

COMFORT FOOD

Sometimes you just need quick bite. Sometimes you want a good meal without too high of a price tag. Whatever the case, Key West has a wide range of casual restaurants to fulfill your need to eat.

ABBONDANZA

(1208 Simonton St. ☎ 305.292.1199) Heaping plates of pasta for a low price is the draw to this restaurant. The staff is mostly Eastern European, though the menu is purely Italian: Mozzarella in Carozza, Linguine "Pescatore", and Veal Cannelloni, to name a few choices. The outdated décor and lack of atmosphere leaves something to be desired, but the food is decent, and there is a full bar. ($$)

B.O.'S FISH WAGON

(801 Caroline St. ☎ 305.294.9272) Very fresh, delicious fish sandwiches on Cuban bread, peel-and-eat shrimp, homemade chowders, and the like are served out of a window at this funky, open-air shack, which looks like a fisherman's junkyard (in a good way). A big black cat walks around looking for hand-outs or napping on a table. Enjoy a beer or ice tea with your meal. You can sit and watch the people walk by on Caroline Street during the day, or enjoy live music in the evenings. ($)

BOBALU'S

(404 Southard St. ☎ 305.296.1664) Decent Southern fare, Key West-infused soulfood and "New Haven-style" pizza sell out into the late night, thanks to the Green Parrot bar next door. The decor and atmosphere was wisely designed to complement the famous Parrot in every way. There is also a Bobalu's in Big Coppit. ($$)

BRAZA LENA

(421 Caroline St. ☎ 305.432.9440) Hard to miss this restaurant at night with its torches burning. Braza Lena is an authentic churrascaria (Brazilian steakhouse) and does meat like no one else. Traditionally dressed gauchos (meat-carvers) circulate around the abstract-art-decorated dining room. They also have a 50+ item salad-and-side-order bar filled with upscale ingredients. There is another Braza Lena in Islamorada. ($$$)

CAMILLE'S

(1202 Simonton St. ☎ 305.296.4811) Camille's fun, kitschy décor and homespun fare with flair makes many a local willing to overlook the slow, haphazard service. Breakfast is the star here, serving lobster omelets, French toast in Godiva white chocolate sauce, or traditional eggs benedict. There is full bar. They are open for breakfast, lunch, and dinner. ($)

CAROLINE'S

(310 Duval St. ☎ 305.294.7511) This soup, sandwich, and salad shop has outdoor seating on the heart of Duval Street.

Conch fritters and po' boys, pasta, and a delicious cheesecake are served for breakfast, lunch or dinner. They also have a full bar. ($)

LA CREPERIE

(300 Petronia St. ☎ 305.517.6799) This lovely, simple eatery sits among the restaurants and shops of Petronia St. serving sweet or savory crepes, pannini, and ice cream, all handmade by its owners who hail from Brittany. Perfect for a light lunch or dessert away from the madness of Duval Street. $

CROISSANTS DE FRANCE

(816 Duval St. ☎ 305.294.2624) This nice French café and bakery offers fresh-baked breakfast and lunch with shaded outdoor seating. Crepes, quiches, and croissants all served. The attached bakery is a great place to stock up on breads and pastries. ($)

DANTE'S

(951 Caroline St. ☎ 305.293.5123) This sprawling outdoor bar and restaurant has a view of the marina and a gorgeous pool in which customers can take a dip. Belly up to one of two bars with the locals, or sit by the pool and snack on seafood or sandwiches. Kids will love the pool and kiddie menu. ($)

FINNEGAN'S WAKE

(320 Grinnell St. ☎ 305.293.0222) Finnegan's offers Irish-pub-style bar food. Their pizza may be the best on the island, and their menu choices get as lofty as Escargot in Brandy Cream Sauce and Pork Tenderloin in Murphy's Amber. Onion rings and chicken wings are popular for watching sports on the giant T.V. or doing serious time at the long, hardwood bar. ($)

FLAMINGO'S CAFÉ

(703½ Duval St. ☎ 305.295.6411) This friendly "greasy spoon" is open for breakfast and lunch only, serving traditional breakfast plus sandwiches, wraps, and salads. They are child friendly, and do not generally serve alcohol. ($)

FOGARTY'S

(227 Duval St. ☎ 305.294.7525) Fogarty's is frequented by mostly college-aged kids looking for copious amounts of food (and beer) for small amounts of cash. Basic burgers, fries, fish sandwiches, etc. are on the menu, none of it particularly well-prepared. ($)

HARD ROCK CAFÉ

(313 Duval St. ☎ 305.293.0230) The Key West version of this popular chain is in a three-story, Victorian house with a gorgeous balcony. Some of the food offered here has a touch of "Florribean", but it is most burgers, wings, and the like, none of it particularly brilliant. Rock 'n' roll memorabilia include some of Jimmy Buffet's clothing and a guitar, one of Bob Dylan's guitars, a drum signed by The Doors, Nikki Sixx's leather jacket, an autographed vest from Keith Richards, and assorted Beatles stuff. You don't even have to go into the restaurant to enjoy the overpriced gift shop. The outdoor seating allows for great people-watching on Duval Street. ($$)

HARPOON HARRY'S

(832 Caroline St. ☎ 305.294.8744) This small, decent diner by the Historic Seaport has a slightly nautical theme and sells booze, cigarettes, and cigars as well. They are open for breakfast and lunch, and do not take credit cards. ($)

JACK FLATS

(509½ Duval St. ☎ 305.294.7955) Southwestern pub-style grub is served in generous portions at this lively Duval bar and restaurant. Food is available until the early morning hours, making it a popular spot for Duval-crawlers. Nachos, burger, fish-and-chips, buffalo wings and the like make for decent eating between pool games, draft beers, and sports on the bar's televisions. ($/$$)

LOBO'S MIXED GRILL

(5 Key Lime Square ☎ 305.296.5303) This lunch-only spot is easy on the wallet, and offers hot or cold sandwiches, wraps, burgers, nachos, and salads. They have beer and wine—and deliver anywhere in old town. The food is pretty tasty for the price. ($)

JIMMY BUFFET'S MARGARITAVILLE

(500 Duval St. ☎ 305.292.1435) Fans of singer Jimmy Buffet are known as "Parrotheads", and they flock by the dozen to Buffet's Key West restaurant. Though he is rarely in attendance, Buffet's songs are played constantly over the sound system, and memorabilia from the singer's life are on display. Unbelievable amounts of burgers, fries, pizzas, wings, etc., plus plenty of beers and booze are sold here on a daily basis. They feature live music from local bands, and many tourists go here just so they can purchase Margaritaville souvenirs from the busy gift shop. ($$)

NEW YORK PASTA GARDEN

(1075 Duval Square ☎ 305.296.2200) Little Italy-styled sandwiches, pasta, and pizza are the fare at this eatery with outdoor seating in quiet Duval Square. The owner's parrots hang out on the patio, adding a tropical vibe to the setting. Prices are reasonable and portions are generous. They serve breakfast, lunch and dinner. ($$)

PEPE'S CAFÉ

(806 Caroline St. ☎ 305.294.7193) This landmark restaurant, founded in 1909, serves no-frills Cuban-American fare in generous amounts. There is neat memorabilia on the walls, and a charming garden bar in back serving cheap drinks. They are open for breakfast, lunch, and dinner. ($)

RUM BARREL

(528 Front St. ☎ 305.292.7862) Pat Croce riffs on the pirate theme with this restaurant and sports bar offering "Great Grub & Grog" (debatable) in a fun atmosphere. Giant televisions, burgers, munchies, Key West shrimp and other finger-foods abound. There is a great view of the action downtown from the rooftop, and a huge selection of beers at the bar. ($)

RHUMBA'S

(708 Duval St. ☎ 305.295.0910) Cuban-style sandwiches and casual fare are served open-air in this small but comfortable eatery between buildings. Cheap food and bar drinks are the draw, but tourists should be aware of an 18% gratuity included in their check. In past years, Rhumba was synonymous with bad food and slow service, but they recently hired local chef Gary Gordon to overhaul the menu, making Rhumba's worth a second try. ($)

SALSA LOCA

(623-625 Duval St. ☎ 305.292.1865) Located off to the side of Cowboy Bill's Saloon, Salsa Loca has the tastiest enchiladas, fajitas, etc. on the island. They have a great selection of vegetarian entrees,and plenty of frozen drinks, flavored margaritas, and beer to wash it down. You can sit in the colorful outdoor seating area or inside at Cowboy Bill's.($)

SOUTHERNMOST BEACH CAFE

(1405 Duval St. ☎ 305.295.6550) Located right on South Beach, this bistro serves breakfast, lunch and dinner in an open-air, clean and casual setting. Food is simple but well-prepared, and happy hour at the bar features half-priced drinks and cheap but delicious tuna sliders, "pelican" wings and fried calamari. Sip on wine from their comprehensive list or a fruity frozen drink. ($$)

THAI CUISINE

(513 Green St. ☎ 305.294.9424) The name says it all: decent Thai dishes with lots of options for vegetarians as well as a good selection of sushi. They have beer, wine, and sake, and nice outdoor seating. They offer great lunch specials and get pretty busy during the dinner hours. ($)

THE CAFÉ

(509 Southard St. ☎ 305.296.5515) This mostly vegetarian restaurant (there is a bit of fish on the menu) provides generous amounts of healthy, tasty fare. Original artwork fills the wall, and the whole place has a funky, downtown, coffee-shop vibe. They also have a nice selection of organic wines and beers. Lunch and dinner both draw a good-sized crowd. ($)

TWO FRIENDS PATIO

(512 Front St. ☎ 305.296.3124) Open since 1967, Two Friends is more famous for its nightly karaoke than its food. Nonetheless, they serve breakfast, lunch, and dinner in an open-air restaurant. Fried grouper sandwich, barbeque pork ribs, and Cajun shrimp pasta is the sort of thing you'll find here—and a full bar to make you drunk enough to sing. ($$)

UPPER CRUST

(611 Duval St. ☎ 305.293.8890) Gourmet pizza with toppings like baby clam, feta cheese, and artichoke hearts bring pizza-lovers by the dozen. The décor is a little retro. They offer wine and beer, and open daily at noon. Many locals declare this the best pizza on the island. ($)

WILLIE T'S

(525 Duval St. ☎ 305.294.7674) Rowdy and young, the crowd at Willie T's enjoys open-air dining, live music on weekends, and 21 flavors of mojito. Stick-to-your-ribs dishes like conch chowder and fritters, fresh pizzas, local fish, and chicken pot pie are served alongside a selection of pasta and vegetarian dishes. The food is okay, but it's more about the fun, young atmosphere. They are open for lunch and dinner every day. ($)

DINING IN STYLE

If you're looking for a bit more pizzazz with your meal, if you want to make an "evening" out of your dining, then Key West offers some of the best restaurants in the southeast. Some of these are "hip" places, and some offer more classical ambiance.

915

(915 Duval St. ☎ 305.294.4737) Stylish 915 has a sexy staff, slick décor, eclectic menu, and good wine list. Housed in a historic Victorian mansion with prime seating on its wrap-around porches, 915 is a great place to see and be seen. Dishes like their signature tuna dome with apple are always interesting—and don't forget to try one of their excellent desserts, like Earl Grey-infused crème brulee. ($$)

AMBROSIA ✪ Must See!

(1401 Simonton St. ☎ 305.293.0304) Located far from the touristy bustle of lower Duval at the Santa Maria Suites Resort, Ambrosia's sleek, modern-zen style dining room is like nothing else in Key West. Prepare to have all your senses stimulated by sushi and Japanese fare that always packs a "wow" factor in terms of both flavor and presentation. Chef Masa is one of the Keys most dynamic chefs and Ambrosia could rival any restaurant in a much bigger city. The staff is knowledgeable and enthusiastic and the sake bar is a great spot for lounging. Expect a wait during prime dining hours. ($$)

ANTONIA'S ✪ Must See!

(615 Duval St. ☎ 305.294.6565) Regional recipes from Tuscany are given upscale flair and served in a huge, gorgeous dining room. The waitstaff shows equal attention to detail, making this a great dining experience all around. They have a massive wine list, and are open for lunch and dinner. ($$$)

AZUR

(425 Grinnell St. ☎ 305.292.2987) This hidden local's favorite features Mediterranean cuisine in an elegant setting for breakfast, lunch, and dinner. Chef-owners Michael Mosi and Drew Wenzel are the genuine artifacts, both boasting experience cooking Tuscan, German and Italian fare. The menu is small and well chosen with meats and seafoods running the show. The wine list is complimentary. Look for the Eden House on Fleming St.: Azur is attached. ($$$)

BAGATELLE

(115 Duval St. ☎ 305.296.6609) Bagatelle offers French-inspired fare among the hustle and bustle of Duval Street. The wraparound porches are great for people watching, and the downstairs bar attracts many locals who come for their martinis. The food is hit-or-miss, despite the fine-dining price. ($$/$$$)

BANANA CAFÉ

(1211 Duval St. ☎ 305.294.7227) Breakfast, lunch and dinner with a French twist. Delicious crepes, a solid, French-inspired brunch and lunch and excellent dinner entrees draw steady crows in this casual indoors-or-out bistro on the subdued end of Duval Street. Enjoy a nice view of several galleries and shops while you eat. ($$)

BLACKFIN BISTRO

(918 Duval St. ☎ 305.509.7408) Breakfast, lunch and dinner is served in this classic bistro offering a blend of French and American fare. Located on the quiet upper end of Duval, the food at Blackfin is uncomplicated and well-prepared. Inside, the tables are crowded close together, but there is outdoor seating in the courtyard. ($$)

BETTER THAN SEX ✪ Must See!

(411 Petronia St. ☎ 305.296.8102) This sinfully dark and sexy dessert bordello offers decadent sweets paired with delicious wines. These unique and delicious designer desserts are truly arousing to the senses, and the staff will enthusiastically point you toward their favorites. They are open from Wednesday through Sunday 6 p.m. to 1 a.m. ($$)

BLUE HEAVEN ✪ Must See!

(729 Thomas St. ☎ 305.296.8666) It's not about the food here, which is fine, but it's about the Key West-y-ness of it all. Located in the largely un-gentrified neighborhood of Bahama Village, Blue Heaven is away from the tacky vibe of Duval Street and has laid-back Caribbean atmosphere to spare. Sit in the airy, shady courtyard with cats and chickens roaming at your feet while you eat under gigantic coconut trees. Some nights feature live musicians or maybe even a play. The food has a southwestern flare and they have good wines. They serve lunch, brunch, and dinner. ($$)

CAFÉ MARQUESA

(600 Fleming St. ☎ 305.294.1117) This is one of the priciest restaurants on the island. Chef Susan Ferry studied under celebrity chef Norman Van Aken, who used to have a restaurant in Key West. This is classic fine dining with sort of a French Caribbean feel. Local "foodies" feel that food is outdated, and Ferry has fallen back on her reputation. Still, Marquesa has many, many fans. There is nice wine bar in the corner if you just want to take a look. ($$$)

CAFÉ SOLE

(1029 Southard St. ☎ 305.294.0230) Chef John Correa and wife Judy offer a taste of Provence-meets-Key West with dishes like Conch Carpaccio, Grouper Romesco, or Filet Mignon "Casa Nova." The décor is French-countryside cozy, and the wine list is thoughtful. They offer dinner year-round, and have great lunch deals during the winter. ($$)

COLUMBIAN GRACE

(223 Petronia St. ☎ 305.240.1281) Breakfast, lunch and dinner are served indoors or outdoors in this spacious and stylish restaurant run by a real Columbian native. The food is delicious and stick-to-your ribs, complemented by beer, wine, or sangria. The balcony overlooking Bahama Village is great for people-watching. ($$)

FLAMING BUOY FILET CO.

(1100 Packer St. ☎ 305.295.7970) Though off the beaten path, Flaming Buoy is a fun, hip neighborhood restaurant serving a small, eclectic "Florribean" menu complemented by a fantastic wine list. There are only a handful of tables packed rather close together. The vibe is personable is casual, and the staff and owners are quick to match wits with the mostly local clientele. ($$)

GRAND CAFÉ

(314 Duval St. ☎ 305.292.4740) The Grand sits elegantly overlooking Duval, serving fine-dining fare like pan-seared sea scallops in Key Lime Buerre Blanc, wild mushroom fettuccini, or a traditional "surf and turf." They have a more-than-decent wine list, full bar, and attentive service. The quality of the food doesn't necessarily reflect the price—but the historic Grand is one of the most expensive pieces of real estate on the island. ($$$)

HOT TIN ROOF

(0 Duval St. ☎ 305.296.7701) Enjoy "Conch Fusion" cuisine in an elegant dining room overlooking the Gulf of Mexico. Paella, Shrimp Creole, and Roqeufort-crusted filet mignon are all on the menu. Service is attentive, and there is a full bar and wine list. They are open for dinner only. ($$$)

KELLY'S

(303 Whitehead St. ☎ 305.293.8484) Actress Kelly McGillis (of Top Gun and Witness fame) owns this Caribbean-flavored restaurant. It has lovely garden seating and stuff made out of airplanes. Jerked chicken, yellowtail snapper with mojo verde, and Island Paella are options. Enjoy one of a selection of micro-brew beers, fine wines, or specialty drinks. They are open for lunch and dinner. ($$)

LATTITUDES

(Sunset Key ☎ 305 292 5394) Though Lattitudes is not exactly in Key West, it is accesible only by a ferry which leaves from behind the Westin. A ten minute boat ride brings you to Sunset Key and this restaurant on the beach. A romantic setting, excellent food and solicitous staff makes Lattitudes popular with newlyweds and for other special occasions. Once on the island, you are not allowed to do anything except go to the restaurant unless you are a guest or resident of Sunset Key Guest Cottages. You will be issued a pass for the ferry when you make reservations. ($$$)

LA TRATTORIA

(524 Duval St. ☎ 305.296.1075) Great old-world Italian fare by candlelight is served in this romantic, bustling restaurant. The wine and martini lists are extensive, and reservations are a must. Afterwards, step into the attached Virgilio's for some great jazz music, dancing, and cocktails. ($$$)

LOUIE'S BACKYARD ✪ Must See!

(700 Waddell St. ☎ 305.294.1061) Off the proverbial beaten path, elegant Louie's overlooks the ocean and serves delicious American cuisine that is refined without being fussy. They are open for lunch and dinner with a fantastic wine list. Louie's afterdeck is one of the best-kept secrets on the island, where you can have a great glass of wine or cocktail in the moonlight on a beautiful wooden floor over the ocean. ($$$)

MAISON DE PEPE ✪ Must See!

(410 Wall St. ☎ 305.295.2690) In Mallory Square, with indoor/outdoor seating, Maison has one foot in the Sunset Celebration madness. It is generally boisterous with people having a great time and enjoying some great food. Stick-to-your ribs, fresh, delicious Cuban cuisine is coupled with live salsa music and dancing among décor that reflects the history of Cuba. This place has a great Key West vibe—probably

Dining and Drinking

because everyone there is on vacation. Have Mojito or an El Presidente or something fruity and tropical to drink. They serve lunch and dinner. ($$)

MANGIA MANGIA

(900 Southard St. ☎ 305.294.2469) Imaginative pasta dishes, gorgeous garden seating, and a great wine list are the reasons to go. The pasta is made fresh, and the atmosphere is friendly and relaxed. Do a simple mix-and-match of pasta with your favorite sauce, or try one of the "house specialties," like Picadillo Pasto, Fettucine con Salmone Affumicato, or Bollito Misto di Mare. ($$)

MANGOES

(700 Duval St. ☎ 305.292.4606) Mangoes patio dining area under shady umbrellas is great place to sit and watch the action on Duval Street. Their Caribbean-styled menu features dishes like Mango Chicken and Thai Black Grouper. The long bar and longtime bartender T. K. attract plenty of locals. They serve and lunch and dinner plus a light late-night menu that runs until the early morning hours. ($$)

MARTIN'S

(917 Duval St. ☎ 305.295.0111) Sophisticated and European, Martin's dining room doubles as a lounge complete with DJ after dinner hours. The crowd here is attractive and worldly, and the menu is German and offers tapas for those more interested in lounging than dining. They offer a fantastic selection of cheese, chocolate, wine, and martinis. ($$$)

MICHAEL'S

(532 Margaret St. ☎ 305.295.1300) Michael's is best known for its Prime beef and its fun fondue pots served at the bar. The restaurant itself is airy and comfortable, and service is impeccable. Many people complain that the food doesn't merit the price, but the restaurant is usually packed anyway. ($$$)

OLD TOWN MEXICAN CAFÉ

(609 Duval St. ☎ 305.296.7500) Decent burritos, fajitas, etc., are served in an outdoor setting overlooking Duval. They offer great frozen drinks and seafood specials, and aren't afraid of heat and spice. The crowd is a mixture of locals and tourists, and they are open for lunch and dinner. ($$)

ORIGAMI

(1075 Duval Square ☎ 305.294.0092) Fresh, well-prepared sushi and Japanese dishes are served outdoors (mostly—there are a few tables inside). There's a good selection of traditional Japanese fare, plus a few interesting Key-West creations. A full bar with a good wine, beer, and sake collection completes the experience. They serve dinner only. ($$)

PRIME 951

(951 Caroline St. ☎ 305.296.4000) This restaurant is hidden above Dante's overlooking the seaport. The décor is jazzy and masculine. They offer Prime aged beef offered on individual butcher blocks, plus assorted seafood dishes. They have a full bar and a more-than-decent wine list, and are open for dinner only. ($$$)

ROOFTOP CAFÉ

(310 Front St. ☎ 304.294.2042) Chef Brendan Orr serves up Southwestern fare with a hint of Caribbean for brunch, lunch, and dinner. Its second-story porch overlooks the street in front of Mallory Square, where there's always something to see. The full bar and wine list adds plenty of spunk to this laid-back eatery. The ambiance is homey and relaxed. ($$)

SANTIAGO'S BODEGA

(207 Petronia St. ☎ 305.296.7691) Located in Bahama Village, this small, tapas-style restaurant is influenced by the cuisines of Spain, Greece, and the Mediterranean. The décor is warm and comfortable, and the wine list is excellent. Friends share small plates of yellow fin ceviche, warmed dates stuffed with goat cheese, and prosciutto and provolone croquettes. Santiago's offers plenty of vegetarian options, with the same menu serving as both lunch and dinner. The food here is always fresh and simple, but put together exactly right. ($$)

SARABETH'S

(530 Simonton St. ☎ 305.293.8181) Casual, upscale comfort food like Lemon Ricotta Pancakes for breakfast, Velvety Cream of Tomato Soup for lunch, and Green Chile Pepper Macaroni & 3-Cheese for dinner are served in this lovely historic building. They have indoor or outdoor seating, a full bar, and a small but adequate wine list. ($$)

SQUARE ONE ✪ Must See!

(1075 Duval Square ☎ 305.296.4300) Chef Andrew Nguyen brings innovative world flavors to Square One's contemporary American cuisine. This is old-school fine dining at its best, but with a gay-friendly, island-y sense of fun. Square One is frequented by loyal, long-time Key Westers and visitors who return season after season. Charming owner Michael Stewart is almost always at the door to greet you, and fixture bartender Patty will whip you up some "Monkey Nuts." Lunch and brunch are a great deal, and arteseanal pizzas are offered at the bar.($$$)

THAI LIFE FLOATING RESTAURANT ✪ Must See!

(1801 m/ Roosevelt Blvd, City Marina ☎ 305.296.9907) Located in New Town in the City Marina, Thai Life is not to be confused with Thai Island, the other Thai restaurant located next door to Garrison Bight. Thai Life imitates the traditional boat-restaurants of Thailand and is the only one of its kind in the U.S. The chef-owner, Dow Lowe, came to Key West after losing everything in the tsunami. Her Thai cuisine is genuine, delicious, and the best of the three Thai restaurants on the island. She will accommodate requests whenever possible. Small, not crowded, and mostly locals, this is a great spot to watch for manatee who frequently swim into the marina. They serve lunch and dinner and are closed on Tuesdays. ($$)

TURTLE KRAALS

(231 Margaret St. ☎ 305.294.2640) Seaport-side, open-air ultra-casual dining with a Southwestern flair is offered for breakfast, lunch, and dinner. A mesquite smoker is utilized on all manner of meats and there are also plenty of seafood choices. The portions are huge and the stick-to-your ribs food is consistently good. There is sports on the televisions around the bar. ($)

SEAFOOD STARS

You can't read or hear about Key West (or the Florida Keys) without being told about the plethora of fantastic seafood restaurants. As is to be expected, seafood couldn't be any fresher. It goes with the territory. When you're on an island paradise, seafood possibilities are everywhere.

A&B LOBSTER HOUSE

(700 Front St. ☎ 305.294.5880) This sprawling dining room above Alonzo's Oyster Bar overlooks the seaport and has outdoor seating as well. Lobster and other seafood are given white-linen service. The food is elegantly simple and well-prepared. There is an adjoining cocktail and cigar bar for after dinner. This restaurant is dinner only. ($$$)

ALONZO'S OYSTER BAR

(700 Front St. ☎ 305.294.5880) Alonzo's offers heaping plates of seafood in a casual setting with indoor or outdoor seating. Alonzo's overlooks the seaport, and offers happy hour at its full bar. Coconut Fried Grouper, Grilled Shrimp and Mashers, and, of course, oysters, peel-and-eat shrimp, and Florida lobster are part and parcel of this mainly seafood menu. Alonzo's has one of the island's best happy hour deals, featuring half-priced drinks and appetizers from 4:30 to 6:30 p.m. daily. ($$)

COMMODORE

(700 Front St. ☎ 305.294.9191) Next to A&B Lobster House, also overlooking the waterfront, the Commodore has a beautiful dining room. Seafood and steaks are on the menu, as are many fine wines and a full bar. Prices are hefty, but competitive with nearby restaurants of the same caliber. ($$$)

CONCH REPUBLIC SEAFOOD COMPANY

(631 Greene St. ☎ 305.294.4403) This boisterous, open-air restaurant overlooks the seaport, has a tropical fish tank running the length of the bar, and often features live music. Baked Oysters Callaloo, fresh local catch, and a selection of Caribbean-inspired pasta dishes are served for lunch and dinner. They have a full raw bar and happy hour daily. "The Conch Farm," as it is often called by locals, has one of the most popular happy hours on the island with two for one drinks. ($$)

DUFFY'S STEAK & LOBSTER HOUSE

(1007 Simonton St. ☎ 305.296.4900) Duffy's is the sort of generic restaurant you'll find in any seaside town. It has little to distinguish it, but you get what you came for: fresh lobster from Maine or Florida, big cuts of Filet Mignon or T-bone, and all the expected side orders. There is a full bar, and they open for lunch and dinner. ($$)

JACK'S SEAFOOD SHACK

(420 Duval St. ☎ 305.296.2991) At the La Concha Hotel, Jack's Seafood offers decently priced, but unexceptional seafoods and sandwiches. The set up is a bit odd as the kitchen is far from the dining room and the bathrooms are actually in the hotel. The staff tends to be hit-or-miss in terms of service. Generally, locals don't go here so expect to encounter only other tourists and hotel guests. You will get much fresher seafood at any of the restaurants along the waterfront. ($$)

Dining and Drinking

HALF SHELL RAW BAR ✪ Must See!

(231 Margaret St. ☎ 305.294.7496) The fish is super-fresh at this funky fish-shack. License plates line the walls, and patrons sit at picnic tables with rolls of paper towels in the center. Have your oysters raw or cooked, try some Key West shrimp or local fish, or enjoy something off the daily specials board. Raw bar is loud and crowded, offering a great view of the seaport. They have a full bar, open for lunch and dinner. ($/$$)

PISCES

(1007 Simonton St. ☎ 305.294.7100) Enjoy classical fine dining fare while gazing upon original Warhol artworks. Beluga caviar, grouper braised in champagne, and filet mignon are a few of the fineries offered here. An elegant wine list completes the experience. They serve dinner only. ($$$)

RED FISH, BLUE FISH

(407 Front St. ☎ 305.295.7747) Fried fish dishes are the main fare at this open-air eatery next to Mallory Square. Mainly frequented by tourists, Red Fish, Blue Fish is rustic and salty, with food that's nothing special, open for breakfast through dinner. They offer a full bar with tropical frozen drinks. ($/$$)

SCHOONER WHARF BAR

(202 William St. ☎ 305.292.9520) The bar and live music are the reason people go, but there is bar food too. They serve breakfast, lunch, and dinner. Nachos, sandwiches, "galley plates," and a raw bar compliment cheap drinks and a friendly crowd. Seating is outside, and there are two "happy hours" daily! ($)

SEVEN FISH ⭐ Must See!

(632 Olivia St. ☎ 305.296.2777) Tables are crowded close together, city-style, at this hip little tropical bistro hidden away from the chaos of Duval Street. The eclectic menu offers wild mushroom quesadillas or vegetable spring Rolls, penne pasta with mango chutney and crawfish or banana chicken with carmalized walnuts. Seven Fish is open for dinner only. ($$)

BARS & CLUBS

Drinking is a popular pastime in Key West, and there are plenty spots devoted to it. Even if you don't indulge, the taverns are great places to meet locals and other travelers or listen to live music. There is almost never a cover charge to go inside, and dancing is usually encouraged.

Technically, you are not allowed to walk down the street with an open container of booze. However, it is generally understood that everyone looks the other way if the drink is in a plastic cup. But don't act like wasted jerk, or the cops can use the "open container" law to arrest you. Some places are not okay with you bringing in booze from another bar—they want you to buy their liquor.

We have included gay bars and clubs in their own section, but plenty of gay people go to the other bars too—and often straights hang out at the gay bars. Many bars do allow smoking. Luckily, there are lots of open-air saloons, or bars with outdoor seating.

BEAR BOTTOM BEACH CLUB

(218 Duval St. ☎ 305.292.0486) Live music, pizza, and other bar-type snacks are the draws to this touristy spot. Giant televisions show "the game" on event nights. The beer is cold, and the crowd is young and drunk.

BOTTLECAP

(1128 Simonton St. ☎ 305.296.2807) A little bit country, and a little bit rock-n-roll, this local's bar is away from hectic Duval. It has cozy, lounge-y corners, a dance floor, pool table, and all the popcorn you can eat. The entertainment, be it live music or a DJ, tends to be hit-or-miss.

BULL & WHISTLE

(224 Duval St. ☎ 305.296.4565) You can't miss this huge, friendly, open-air pub with the giant bull's head out front. Downstairs has a stage featuring mostly second-rate musicians, but upstairs has a great wrap-around porch for people watching on Duval Street, plus bar games and good music on the sound system.

CAPTAIN TONY'S ✪ Must See!

(428 Greene St. ☎ 305.294.1838) Originally an ice-house which doubled as the town morgue, this historic building has a colorful history as a cigar factory, bordello, and speakeasy. This pub, known for it's ice-cold beers and live music, bills itself as the oldest bar in Key West (since 1933!) It was the site of the original "Sloppy Joe's," which was a hangout of Hemingway (he met his third wife here). Later, Jimmy Buffet performed here regularly. It's a dark, grungy cave with lots of character, historical mementos, and a "hangin' tree" growing right through the roof (in the 1800's, 17 pirates were hung from this tree by vigilantes). Speaking of dead bodies, the coroner's daughter is still buried under the pool table.

CHARTROOM

(1 Duval St. ☎ 305.296.4600 x477) This quirky, friendly, tiny bar has peanut shells on the floor and all the popcorn you can eat. It is hidden away inside the Pier House resort, but that doesn't stop locals from sneaking in. Enjoy buttery popcorn from the popcorn machine while you drink.

CORK AND STOGIE

(1218 Duval St. ☎ 305.517.6419) This laid-back wine-and-cigar bar in an old house lets you smoke and drink on the porch while people-watching on upper Duval. They offer discounts to cruise ship passengers.

COWBOY BILL'S

(628 Duval St. ☎ 305.293.7663) Cowboy Bill's is the Keys' only honky tonk, and it is huge, with three bars, a restaurant, several televisions, pool tables and games, a dance floor, and a mechanical bull! They have a great 2 for 1 happy hour with half-priced appetizers. They often feature live country music — and did I mention the mechanical bull?

CROW'S NEST

(208 Duval St. ☎ 305.296.4890) You might mistake this for the second floor of Rick's, but technically, it's another bar. From up there, you can watch the bands at Rick's or the people below. It's a less-hectic retreat from the noise and crowd of Rick's and Durty Harry's.

DON'S PLACE

(1000 Truman St. ☎ 305.296.8837) Don's is well off the beaten path of Duval, and locals love it. An assorted cast of Key West characters mixes it up at two bars — one inside, one out. There are pool tables and foosball and other games. They close for only three hours, in the wee morning.

DURTY HARRY'S

(208 Duval St. ☎ 305.296.4890) This loud, crowded, gritty sports bar / rock club has 15 televisions, and the best, loudest, rock bands on the island. The crowd is young and rowdy, and there are two bars to keep you drinking.

EL ALAMO

(4 Charles St. ☎ 305 517 6350) This friendly, rowdy, outdoor bar attracts twentysomethings with live rock and regaee, sexy shots girls, and cheap drinks. Partiers can dance on the ground in front of the stage, take a seat at the giant bar, or play cornhole and other outdoor bar games.

FAT TUESDAY

(305 Duval St. ☎ 305.296.9373) When MTV filmed *The Real World* in Key West, this was the bar where the cast most often played out their drunken dramas. It is open-air with loud music and lots of young tourists trying to pick each other up. They have a huge selection of fruity frozen drinks.

GARDEN OF EDEN

(224 Duval St. ☎ 305.296.4565) Above the Bull & Whistle is the clothing-optional Garden of Eden. It is located on a gorgeous rooftop overlooking Duval, with lots of potted plants where you can hide or a dance floor where you can let it all show! There is usually only a handful of nudies and lots of clothed onlookers, but that is enough to create a loose, slightly surreal vibe. They play great dance music, and offer body painting in a discreet corner behind screens.

GRAND VIN

(1107 Duval St. ☎ 305.296.1020) Get away from the kids chugging beer on lower Duval and sit on an elegant porch with an excellent glass of wine. This is the only place in Key West that serves "flights", so you can compare and contrast three different wines from the same region, or of the same variety, etc. Locals love it here, but tourists are welcome as well.

GREEN PARROT ✪ Must See!

(601 Whitehead St. ☎ 305.294.6133) This is the quintessential Key West bar, frequented by locals and tourists alike. They have incredible blues, jazz, funk, and rock bands, and a great jukebox for when the bands are on break. The building is historic, dating back to the 1880s. There's pool and pinball, and a souvenir shop attached. There is no glass in the windows, keeping the place airy and tropical.

GRUNTS

(409 Caroline St. ☎ 305.294.8280) This sleepy wine bar with rustic indoor lounge or spacious outdoor seating is a nice way to get away from the crazyness of nearby Duval St. They also have beer.

HISTORIC CIGAR ALLEY

(1075 Duval Square ☎ 305.294.2224) People are often drawn in by the unforgetable face of the proprieters' old English bulldog, Duke. They stay for a great selection of boutique wines and cigars. Historic Cigar has the largest walk-in humidifier in Key West. You can either sit at the bar and chat with the owners, Chris and Becky, or sit on a sofa and watch sports, or play dominoes.

HOG'S BREATH SALOON

(400 Front St. ☎ 305.292.2032) This is one of Key West's most famous hangouts, featuring great blues and rock bands, a rowdy crowd of locals and tourists, and even burgers, oysters, and fish sandwiches to soak up the booze. You will hear Hog's Breath before you see it — and there is always a crowd dancing and carrying on in this cozy, open-air love shack.

IRISH KEVIN'S

(211 Duval St. ☎ 305.292.1262) Live music keeps this Irish-style pub loud and crowded. They feature Guinness-chugging contests and two televisions showing sports. There is a lot of cursing and lewd behavior — especially as the night progresses.

ISLAND DOGS

(505 Front St. ☎ 305.295.0501) This newly-opened bar also serves light food. They have decent DJs or live music in a sophisticated but casual, lounge-like atmosphere. Or, you can sit out front and people-watch.

LAZY GECKO

(203 Duval St. ☎ 305.292.1903) Lazy Gecko is filled with
drinking college-aged guys in baggy shirts and baseball caps —
perhaps because of the sexy female bartenders, who have been
known to dance on the bar. Loud and crowded and filled with
tourists, the Gecko has DJs or live music nightly.

RED GARTER

(208 Duval St. ☎ 305.296.4890) Great-looking girls bare all
in this strip club in the heart of the Duval Street bar scene.
Men and women are both welcome here with no cover charge.
The club takes up an entire floor of the Rick's/Durty Harry
complex and is always rocking. These are the best-looking
strippers on the island. Please note you WILL be thrown
out for drug use, harassing, or laying hands on the girls. No
excuses, no second chances.

RICK'S

(208 Duval St. ☎ 305.296.4890) Rick's is Key West's only real
nightclub, and is a part of the "Rick's complex" with Durty
Harry's and the Crows Nest. It is frequented by young tourists and locals, mostly looking to hook up for the night but
not before hitting the dancfloor to current pop and dance hits.
Dancing and partying to the wee hours of the night is what
Rick's is all about..

RUM RUNNER'S HOUSE

(1117 Duval St. ☎ 305.296.2680) On the quiet end of Duval
Street, this low-key little bar below the Speakeasy Inn has an
impressive list of rums as well as other premium liquors. Sit
inside at the intimate bar or pull up a chair outside on the

porch. This is a local's favorite, but enough tourists come by to keep it interesting. They also have a fine selection of cigars and a mellow old cat who hangs out with patrons on the porch. This is a great spot for people-watching along upper Duval.

SUNSET PIER

(0 Duval St. ☎ 305.295.7045) For a fantastic view of the Gulf of Mexico, head out onto the pier and sit on one of the colorful barstools at Sunset Pier. They also serve decent, if overpriced, bar food, and often feature very good live music. This is a great place to see Key West's famous sunsets without braving the madness on Mallory Square.

SLOPPY JOE'S

(201 Duval St. ☎ 305.294.5717) Open at that location since 1937, Sloppy Joe's features Hemingway memorabilia, live music, dancing, and overpriced food (including a Sloppy Joe sandwich). The Backroom has satellite TV and porch seating; and the Speak Easy, located upstairs, offers balcony seating over looking Greene Street, and satellite TV. It is very popular with tourists.

SPORT'S PAGE BAR AND GRILL

(610 Greene St. ☎ 305.296.3230) The name says it all: sports on television sets, decent burgers and chicken wings, happy hour daily and no-frills. The prices are reasonably low despite its prime downtown real estate.

TEASERS

(218 Duval St. ☎ 305.292.0486) Go upstairs from the Bear Bottom Beach Club to see real bear bottoms. Get a private dance or buy a bottle of champagne and see what happens in the champagne room. Women can come in too.

THE PORCH

(429 Caroline St.) Taking up one large room and a part of the verandah of the old Porter Mansion, the Porch serves a thoughtful selection of microbrewed beers, affordable-but-excellent wines, and real root beer for non-drinkers. The atmosphere is casually elegant with a sense of humor: kung-fu movies play on the flatscreen while the drink menus have photos from kitchy movies. The acoustics inside make the place seem even louder and more crowded than it really is. Having just opened in summer of 2010, The Porch remains undiscovered by most tourists, and fills nightly with friendly locals.

UPSTAIRS AT MANGOES

(700 Duval St. ☎ 305.292.4606) On Friday and Saturday nights, Mango's restaurant opens its upstairs as a late-night dance club complete with state-of-the-art sound and light systems and world-class DJs. This is a locals hotspot where Key Westers dance until dawn.

VIRGILIO'S ✪ Must See!

(524 Duval St. ☎ 305.296.8118) Sophisticated without taking itself too seriously, Vigilio's is a quirky, cool jazz club. Enjoy the cozy garden bar with the tree (decorated with mannequin legs) growing through the middle, or get down on the dance floor. They have a great selection of beers, wines, martinis and specialty drinks. The crowd is a diverse mix of locals and tourists from all walks of life. They even serve late-night snacks from the kitchen of the attached Italian restaurant. Drinks here are pricey (except on "Martini Mondays") but very well-made and well-presented.

WHITE TARPON

(700 Front St. ☎ 305.295.5222) Looking over the Seaport, this little wine-and-martini bar in a liquor store is a local favorite, frequented by boaters who park in the marina below and oenophiles who enjoy being able to grab a bottle to go (while watching the food channel on the television set behind the bar. Try their Key Lime Martini with graham cracker rim.

WORLD'S SMALLEST BAR

(124 Duval St. ☎ 305.294.8507) This adorable little hole-in-the-wall seats about four people comfortably. Chat with the friendly bartenders and watch Duval Street go by. The selection is small here also; so don't ask for much beyond the basics.

GAY BARS

Key West's gay culture, and in particular the bar and nightlife scene, is arguably the most popular in America. Many visitors and locals will argue that there is no point in giving these establishments their own section in a travel guide. Key West visitors love to "mix it up."

801 BOURBON

(801 Duval St. ☎ 305.296.1992) This charming dive with an adorable stage offers drag cabarets nightly, and is a decent mix of locals and tourists, gay, straight, and transsexual. Leave your hang-ups outside and enjoy hanging out at either bar, upstairs or down. Saloon 1, in the back, is for men only, and features gay "adult entertainment" on four televisions and lots of guys cruising.

BOURBON STREET PUB

(724 Duval St. ☎ 305.296.1992) This is where the boys are. Two bars inside, one out back by the pool, a giant television, dance music, and hot go-go boys make the scene steamy. Women are allowed, but this is definitely a boys' club.

AQUA 711 ✪ Must See!

(Duval St. ☎ 305.294.0555) It is tough to miss this open-front club, which uses it's floor/stage for live music, drag cabarets, karaoke, or dancing, depending on which night you're going. The crowd is mixed gay, lesbian, and straight. The bartenders often perform as well, making for an entertaining evening.

BOBBY'S MONKEY BAR

(900 Simonton ☎ 305.294.2655) Step off of Duval and enjoy this utterly unpretentious, quirky neighborhood pub where everyone seems to know everyone else. They have Karaoke on most nights—and the people who sing take it very seriously! There's a pool table, television screens, a jukebox, and computerized games.

KWEST

(705½ Duval St. ☎ 305.292.6706) Go-go guys dance after 10 p.m. Early evenings are more about showtunes and lounging by the piano. Live music and shows are offered frequently. The clientele is mostly men, but women and straight couples are often around in the early evening.

LA TE DA

(1125 Duval St. ☎ 305.296.6706) La Te Da has fantastic cabaret shows on its stage upstairs, like their famous "Broadway Three-Ways" or the best female impersonators in the Keys. Downstairs, enjoy live music at the piano, or check out their restaurant and pool.

PEARL'S PATIO BAR

(525 United St. ☎ 305.292.1450) This is the only lesbian bar on the island. It's inside Pearl's Rainbow resort, and attracts a good mix of local women and tourists. Happy hour is the best time to go.

The Arts in Key West

✪

Duval Street is overrun with tacky tee-shirt shops and tawdry souvenir stores; if you want a real keepsake to remember the island, you should visit the art galleries. For such as small town, Key West has an incredible number of talented artists among its citizens. Many galleries feature contemporary paintings and sculpture from around the world as well as local talent.

The island also has inordinately good theater, film, and music. If you're coming from a big city like New York or Boston, you might not be impressed, but Key West's arts scene is better than most towns of similar size--without big city prices. Seeing a play, watching a film, or listening to an orchestra in Key West is always a unique experience, as the island adds its own personality to everything, even the arts.

GALLERIES

Artists and art enthusiasts flock to Key West for inspiration, for promotion, and for meeting their fellows. It is a place teeming with creativity, and there is no shortage of galleries where the local and nationally famous alike can meet to display (and sell) their one-of-a-kind works.

7 ARTISTS

(604 Duval St. ☎ 305.293.0411) This gallery is actually a co-op of the artists and artisans who show there, and one of them is always on site, working the phones and cash register while they work their medium. They offer sculptures, paintings, prints,

glassware, and jewelry, mostly with a tropical flair. The crafts
here are surprisingly affordable and make great keepsakes and
conversation pieces.

1100 SODU

(1100 Duval St. ☎ 305.296.4400) This new gallery features
woodwork, jewelry, sculpture, paintings, prints, and pottery by
six local artists. The space itself is bright, colorful, and airy.
The art here is affordable, if not always remarkable.

ALAN S. MALTZ GALLERY ✪ Must See!

(1210 Duval St. ☎ 305.294.0005) Maltz's stunning photographs of Florida Keys' wildlife and architecture are beautiful
in a garish sort of way. His captures are almost Technicolor,
the way they exaggerate and exacerbate the amber glow of
dawn, the soft pink of a bird's feathers, or the red of a hotel's
awning. He has published two coffee-table books full of
photos that will have to do if you can't afford an original (the
smallest, unframed picture is barely under $1,000).

A BOY AND HIS DOG ✪ Must See!

(826 & 626 Duval St. ☎ 305.296.5567) This gallery consists
of two buildings a block away from each other, and sells
contemporary pop-art (think Andy Warhol), created by living
artists both local and from around the world. Thomas Arvid's
luscious paintings of wine are a local favorite, as are cartoonish
renditions of the Rolling Stones, Jimi Hendrix, and other pop
icons.

GALLERY KEY WEST

(824 Duval St. ☎ 305.292.0046) Paintings, plateware, jewelry, photography, and stained glass are sold here. All are from local artists, and very well done. This gallery mixes a pop-art sensibility with a tropical island feel. The work here is generally quite affordable and of high quality.

GALLERY ON GREENE

(606 Greene St. ☎ 305.292.0046) This spacious gallery displays paintings by local artists past and present. Mostly, the selection is paintings of Key West scenery, but there is also some more innovative work. On display are Mario Sanchez's woodcarvings, cartoonist Jeff McNally's humorous paintings, and Suzie Depoo Zuzek's work with ceramics and driftwood.

GINGERBREAD SQUARE GALLERY ✪ Must See!

(1207 Duval St. ☎ 305.296.8900) This gallery claims to be Key West's oldest (33 years!) and features paintings, sculptures, and art glass by local and international artists. The building is a charming Victorian mansion. The artwork itself reflects Key West / tropical island themes, but beautifully, imaginatively rendered. The work here is high-caliber, with prices to reflect.

GUILD HALL

(614 Duval St. ☎ 305.296.6076) Guild Hall Gallery is an artists' co-op established in 1976. It is "the oldest Duval Street art gallery in its' original location." Guild Hall provides two floors of affordable space for Key West artists to display their work. There is an assortment of styles and mediums to choose from, and prices vary—from realistic wildlife photos to colorful watercolors of Key West scenes and every kind of work in between.

HAITIAN ART CO.

(600 Frances St. ☎ 305.296.8932) Opened in 1978, this gallery features art purchased from native Haitans in their own country. An incredible amount of objects are in display, including spirit flags, works in wood, stone, metal, and papier-mâché, all sold for a reasonable price.

HARRISON GALLERY

(825 White St. ☎ 305.294.0609) Owned and operated by wood sculptor Helen Harrison, this inviting space features painting, sculpture, and woodwork from local and international artists. The pieces here are realistic and earthy with a tropical / nautical feel. Some pieces are functional, while others are pure art. Harrison's work is always present, and other exhibits change on a rotating basis.

HELIO GARDENS GALLERY

(526 Angela St. ☎ 305.294.7901) This small gallery within the Gardens Hotel features nature-based work from local artists. The emphasis is on affordable, aesthetically-pleasing paintings, sculptures, and ceramics. Formerly located on Fleming Street, the gorgeous, lush setting of the Gardens is a compliment to the artwork.

HERMES GALLERY

(608 Greene St. ☎ 305.296.4550) Paintings, bronze sculptures, stained glass, and other media by mostly local artists. The pieces here are generally island-themed, with styles ranging from photo-realism to modern cubism.

JOY GALLERY

(1124 Duval St. ☎ 305.296.3039) Reasonably priced artwork by both local and international artists is featured at this landmark gallery. The work here is island-themed, mostly realistic in style and content. This is a great place to go for affordable island scenery paintings.

KENT GALLERY

(821 Duval St. ☎ 305.292.5646) Displaying the work of both emerging and internationally known artists, the Kent Gallery features contemporary and abstract paintings, sculpture, photography, and furniture. This gallery is aimed at collectors as well as vacationers looking for an interesting memento.

KEY WEST ART CENTER

(301 Front St. ☎ 305.294.1241) 70 local artists participate in this non-profit gallery, so there's something for everyone. This co-op was established in 1955 and is still going strong. Here, art enthusiasts are frequently able to find quality, affordable artwork to add to their collections.

KW LIGHT GALLERY

(534 Fleming St. ☎ 305.294.0566) Author, photographer, and painter Sharon Wells offers photos, original paintings, giclee prints, posters, etc. The handful of artists who show here are generally unexceptional, but the collection of black and white historic photos showing the Keys and Cuba are nice.

KEY WEST GALLERY

(601 Duval St. ☎ 305.292.9339) Paintings and lithographs
from international artists are sold here. There's some gorgeous
stuff in this gallery, mostly with a nod toward Impressionism,
but also a few prerequisite palm-tree-by-the-beach scenes.
Original painting can get into the tens of thousands of dollars
here, but smaller pieces gicless are more reasonably priced. The
staff is definitely looking for sales and can get a little pushy, but
they are fairly patient with looky-loos.

LEMONADE STAND ART STUDIO

(227 Petronia St. ☎ 305.295.6873) Letty Nowak and Eric
Anfinson create and show their vibrant works here. They are
especially fond of portraits of local characters. The vibe here
is more East Village than Bahama Village, and the Lemonade
Stand, though only a few years old, has quickly become central
to the Key West artistic community. It seems like Letty and
Eric are always up to something interesting: like their annual
"lock-in" where 13 artists shut themselves into the studio for
24 hours together and create work to be displayed afterwards.

LUCKY STREET GALLERY ⭐ Must See!

(1130 Duval St. ☎ 305.294.3973) Gallery owner Diane
Zolotow shows contemporary paintings and sculpture by a
rotating cast of mostly-local artists. This is some of the best
art the island has to offer; sometimes beautiful, sometimes
innovative, and always interesting. Pieces here goes beyond the
sailboat-by-a-palm-tree-on-the-beach scenery seen in much
local work, but still has something uniquely Key West about it
all.

LUIS SOTTIL GALLERY

(716 Duval St. ☎ 305.292.6447) Sottil is the originator of an artistic movement known as "Naturalismo". He paints with natural substances (like 14k gold paint), and using actual rainforest plants and insects. There's also gorgeous work from other international artists here. The staff is knowledgeable and enthusiastic. Prices are high

MONKEY APPLE ART FACTORY

(1022 Duval St. ☎ 305.296.4100) Featuring the bold, colorful still lifes of local artist Susan Guadagno, Monkey Apple produces fun, inexpensive art is the form of high-quality giclees on canvas. Or, purchase a post card of the remarkable, fun paintings Guadagno makes on her iPod..

OH MY GODARD GALLERY ✪ Must See!

(719 Duval St. ☎ 305.292.0911) Key West is the perfect town to house Godard's surreal, cute, drink-inspired paintings of olives dancing around a martini glass, strawberries stripping around a champagne glass, drunk grapes, etc. If Bosch's under-world had a bar and a sense of humor, his paintings might have looked like Godard's.

RED DOOR GALLERY

(812 Caroline St. ☎ 305.296.6628) Affordable, island-inspired artwork is sold at this tiny spot in the Waterfront District. This isn't art of the highest quality, but makes for fun souvenirs. Owner Rene Blais presides.

SIGN OF SANDFORD

(328 Simonton St. ☎ 305.296.7493) Sandford Birdsey's watercolors and painted fabric are on display here. Her paintings of Key West landmarks, water vistas, and street scenes display much joie de vivre. Affordable prints in many sizes are available alongside the originals.

STONE SOUP GALLERY

(519 Fleming St. ☎ 305.296.2080) Bright, island-themed artwork from well-known local artists is sold at this intimate gallery. There's a great chaotic, Key West vibe inside, and the staff is laid-back but friendly.

STUDIOS OF KEY WEST ✪ Must See!

(600 White St. ☎ 305.296.0458) Located at the historical Armory building, the Studios is a local hub of the arts community combining visual arts, theater, and music. They offer workshops, concerts, readings, and symposiums in various art forms, have an artist-in-residence program, and are generally always up to something interesting. The Studios hosts its "Walk on White" monthly, always on a Thursday from 6 to 9 p.m. During this time, TSKW and several galleries on White Street encourage looky-loos to wander in, buy a glass of wine for two bucks, and look around with no pressure to purchase anything more.

SUZY STARFISH

(912 Duval St. ☎ 305.292.6624) Bright, joyful, and slightly kitschy island-themed furniture, artwork, jewelry, and clothing are sold in this fun little store. The work here is affordable and great for gift-giving.

THOMAS KINKADE GALLERY

(335 Duval St. ☎ 305.292.0069) Kinkade is America's most collected living artist, and this gallery displays the best of this "painter of light." An eclectic mix of other international artists shares wall space here as well. The staff is happy to converse with you about any piece—even if you're just looking.

WILD SIDE GALLERY

(1108 Duval St. ☎ 305.296.7800) Wild Side features over 50 "American Artists Inspired by Nature." Paintings, woodwork, glass, and pottery are well-crafted and pricey. The materials involved are usually taken from nature, giving the place an earthy, rustic vibe.

WYLAND GALLERIES ✪ Must See!

(623 & 102 Duval St. ☎ 305.292.4998 & 305.294.5240) Two locations feature marine and wildlife art by Wyland and other environmental artists. The larger gallery is impossible to miss, with its breathtaking fountain of three dolphins at play. Wyland has a gift for celebrating the beauty and grandeur of the amazing creatures that inhabit our seas, and prices are high for these top-notch paintings and sculptures.

ZBYSZEK GALLERY

(1102 Duval St. ☎ 305.296.8030) The zany, hyper-colorful work of husband-and-wife Zbyszek and Tippi Koziol is sold here. Their art is purposefully childish, straddling lines between abstract, surrealism, and folk-art. Paintings are in all different mediums, sizes, and prices.

THEATER AND MUSIC

In Key West, arts are not limited to the fine. Performing arts, live shows, music, and cinema all have their place in this historic hubbub of artistic endeavors.

RED BARN THEATER

(319 Duval St. ☎ 305.296.9911) Built in 1829 as the carriage house to for Key West's Oldest House, the Red Barn has been putting on shows since the 1940s. Utilizing mostly local talent (Red Barn and Waterfront Playhouse shows often have similar cast and crews) Red Barn produces high-quality plays and musicals. Recent hits include The Rocky Horror Show, BatBoy: The Musical, and Lettice and Lovage.

TROPIC CINEMA

(416 Eaton St. ☎ 305.295.9493) The Tropic shows a small but well-picked selection of blockbusters, foreign and independent films in intimate theaters on small screens. But what makes the Tropic Cinema so delightful? Is it the quirky staff and right-at-home clientele, or the gourmet snacks and assortment of spices for your popcorn? Maybe it's the fact that you can get a really great glass of wine there and drink it in the theater!

WATERFRONT PLAYHOUSE

(Mallory Square ☎ 305.294.5015) This intimate theater was originally the icehouse for Porter's Warehouse in the 1880s. Waterfront uses local and imported talent to put on great plays and musicals, often with the same casts and crews you'll find at the Red Barn. Their shows are always top-notch. Recent productions include Urinetown: The Musical, The Glass Menagerie, and The Graduate.

KEY WEST POPS

(⬤ keystix.com) Maestro Vincent Zito brings non-classical orchestra favorites to the Keys. The Pops often brings in big names like Leslie Uggams, Jerry Herman, and Lee Roy Reams, as well as showcasing local talent. Broadway, cabaret, and jazz tunes are generally on the playbill. They generally perform at Tennessee Williams Theatre (at the Florida Keys Community College on Stock Island), or smaller venues around town.

KEY WEST BURLESQUE ✪ Must See!

(⬤ keywestburlesque.com) Key West's most unique, dynamic performers tease and titillate in this world-class burlesque group.   Led by voluptous pin-up girl Tatah Dujour, the burlesque puts on shows in various venues and during parties and holidays. They also host parties around town with crazy themes, such as "Make-out" or "no pants" parties. Whatever your sexual orientation, you will be amused, aroused, and astounded by the talent of these men and women all at the same time.

SOUTH FLORIDA SYMPHONY

(⬤ keystix.com) Led by the electric Sebrina Alfonso, Key West Symphony imports impressive professional musicians to make up its world-class symphony. Generally, the symphony plays either at the Tennessee Williams Theatre (at the Florida Keys Community College on Stock Island,) or else at the Glenn Archer Auditorium at the Key West High School on Flagler Ave. Occasionally, the symphony will do an outdoor performance at Fort Zachary Taylor. These events are so popular, they often end up turning people away. If you're going to try to go, go ridiculously early.

Exploring the Other Keys

The Florida Keys is 106 miles long, consisting of countless tiny islands. Though Key West is a lot of fun, some of the most wonderful things to experience in the Keys are on the other, less developed islands. It is nearly impossible to get lost, as US 1—also known as **Overseas Highway**—is the only artery through the Keys, and you can easily traverse its entirety in a day or less. Don't miss the chance to see all the wonders the Keys have to offer.

Navigating U.S. 1 / Overseas Highway is fairly simple. Destinations are addressed via "Mile Markers" so you have Big Pine Key existing at MM30, Marathon at MM50, Tavernier at MM90, etc,. Then, at the end of the Keys, you come to a national treasure that shouldn't be missed: the Everglades National Park.

The Everglades has an ecosystem unlike any other in the world. These vast wetlands were once sufficiently fed by Lake Okeechobee before it was diked and re-channeled, and much of the wetlands were drained to create farmland and residential areas. In 1947, President Truman declared 1.5 million acres of undeveloped land as the Everglades National Park. Diverse bird populations, splendid wild orchids, and endangered animals such as the manatee, the Florida panther, and the American crocodile are just a few of the wonders residing in the Everglades.

In this chapter, we will list some of the places worth stopping for along your journey through the Keys to the Everglades. The must-sees are highlighted, but don't be afraid to get out and explore on your own. Ask the locals where they like to go.

THE LOWER KEYS

Starting just off Key West, this section points out some of the highlights between Stock Island and Little Duck Key.

KEY WEST GOLF CLUB

(Stock Island, 6450 College Rd ☎ 305.294.5232) This public golf course features 6,500 yards and 18 holes suitable for golfers of various levels of experience. Some holes have unique challenges—like a par 3 played over a thick mangrove field. They have a clubhouse and restaurant on site.

KEY WEST TROPICAL FOREST AND BOTANICAL GARDENS

(Garden, Stock Island, 5210 College Rd ☎ 305.296.1504) The only "frost-free" botanical garden in the Continental U.S. was founded in the 1930's, boasts 7.5 acres, and is home to many threatened and endangered tropical plant species. The bird-and-butterfly watching here is excellent. Enjoy meandering pathways, a butterfly garden, freshwater pond, well-labeled foliage, and instructive pamphlets for self-guided tours. They are currently building a gigantic fresh-water pond that will be visible from the sky, attracting birds as they pass through for migration.

HURRICANE JOE'S / HURRICANE HOLE MARINA

(Restaurant, Stock Island, 5114 Overseas Hwy ☎ 305.294.0200) Joe's is the busy watering hole of many local boaters, right on the Hurricane Hole Marina. The restaurant serves up tasty fried seafood and burgers and cold beers and cocktails, either in the casual dining room or even more-casual dockside. This is a great spot for kayak rentals (Lazy Dog gives a great price and a free map) or boat rentals with easy access to the salt ponds and lots of cool mangroves just offshore.

HOGFISH BAR AND GRILL

(Restaurant, Stock Island, 6810 Front St. ☎ 305.293.4041)
Owner Bobby likes to point out that Hogfish is what Key West used to be—casual, inexpensive, outdoors, filled with local characters enjoying fresh fish and strong drinks. The food here is quite good: favorite menu items include the Hogfish Sandwich, Baja Tacos, and the Lobster BLT. Hogfish overlooks Safe Harbor.

RUSTY ANCHOR

(Restaurant, Stock Island, 5510 3rd Ave ☎ 305.294.2893)
This rough-and-tumble back-road bar and restaurant is no where near the "beaten path." It is where the shrimpers and fishermen go after work for super-fresh seafood in generous portions. Rowdy and local, Rusty Anchor is an interesting look at what Key West used to be like—if you can find it (off 5th Street.)

BOBALU'S SOUTHERN CAFÉ

(Restaurant, Big Coppitt Key, 301 Overseas Hwy ☎ 305.296.1624) At mile marker 10, this family-run, southern-style establishment mostly caters to locals and is cash-only. They also offer very good pizza. The vibe here is warm and friendly, and the décor features a tropical plant nursery and antique tavern paraphernalia.

MANGROVE MAMA'S
(Restaurant, Sugarloaf Key, 19991 Overseas Hwy

☎ **305.745.3030)** At mile marker 21, this quirky, no-frills shack (it used to be a gas pumping station) thinks nothing of serving beer in jelly jars, or letting dogs and cats wander the dining room, which shares space with a small library. Food is basic island fare, and there are some miniature horses out back.

SQUARE GROUPER ✪ Must See!
(Restaurant, Summerland Key, 22658 Overseas Hwy

☎ **305.745.8880)** "Square Grouper" is slang for the bales of marijuana that occasionally washed ashore during the Keys' heyday of drug smuggling. Formerly located in Cudjoe Key, this trendy bistro features imaginative island cuisine at middling prices. The décor has a clean, casual, West Indies feel. (MM22.5 Oceanside)

BOONDOCKS GRILLE & DRAFT HOUSE
(Restaurant & Mini-Golf, Ramrod Key, 27205 Overseas Hwy

☎ **305.872.4094)** This is a great place for the family with an 18-hole mini-golf course (the only one in the Keys), lots of finger foods, and a kiddie menu. They offer karaoke, pool tables, dancing, live bands, and more. The tiki-style dining room is wonderful on cool nights. The food is basic Americana with plenty of seafood options. (MM27.5 Bayside)

LITTLE PALM ISLAND RESORT & SPA
(Resort, Little Torch Key ☎ 305.872.2524) If you're willing to shell out some major dollars, Little Palm is well worth the experience. "The Truman," a 35-foot launch, takes you out to this private island resort. Crushed seashell paths lead you

through lush gardens, where guests enjoy a lagoon-style pool, private beach, Zen meditation room, library, and spa. Their restaurant is award-winning and right on the beach in the most romantic setting imaginable. Children and pets are not allowed. (MM28.5 Gulfside)

PARROTDISE WATERFRONT BAR & GRILLE
(Restaurant, Little Torch Key, 183 Barry Ave ☎ 305.872.2201)
Waterfront dining with a Caribbean flair and tasty tropical drinks are only part of the lure to this spacious eatery. Locals and tourists mix easily, and children are welcome here (there is a kiddie menu). Visitors compliment the view, food, drinks, and service, with prices less than what you'd find for the same thing in Key West. More interestingly, they offer live music and a private beach with hammocks and a volleyball net, plus a tropical fish pond and a shark pond. (MM28.5 Bayside)

BLUE HOLE ✪ Must See!
(Nature Park, Big Pine Key, Key Deer Blvd) Blue hole is a quarry that houses a couple of alligators—the only known gators in the Keys. Ducks, turtles, lots of birdlife, and, of course, iguanas are also on hand. Stick to the observation decks and marked trails for your own safety. American Alligators are a protected species. (MM30.5 Bayside)

KEY DEER REFUGE ✪ Must See!
(Nature Park, Big Pine Key, No Name Key, Key Deer Blvd) This unique endangered species lives no where else in the world except on Big Pine and No Name Key. Key Deer are minia-ture—smaller than some dogs, and have the rare ability to drink salt water when necessary. The best time to spot them is

a dusk or dawn when they come out to forage. Key Deer are used to attention—and, unfortunately, to people feeding them. Though this makes them great photograph subjects, it is also often their demise. All too often, Key Deer lingering at the side of the road looking for handouts get hit by cars. Please drive slowly through Key Deer territory, and resist the urge to touch or feed them. If you can't find the deer driving through the refuge, try No Name Key—there is almost always a group foraging there. (MM30.5 Bayside)

WATSON & MANILLO NATURE TRAILS

(Nature, Big Pine Key, Key Deer Blvd) There are two well-maintained nature trails in the heart of the Key Deer Refuge. Watson is 2/3 mile through pineland habitat, and Manillo is 1/5 mile traversing pine rockland and freshwater wetlands. Numerous signs educate visitors on flora and fauna they might be seeing. Delightfully, you can often walk these trails without ever running into another human being. (MM30.5 Bayside)

NO NAME PUB ✪ Must See!

(Restaurant, No Name Key, N. Watson Blvd ☎ 305.872.9115) Dollar bills line the walls of this fun little bar and restaurant. They make perhaps the best pizza in the Keys, plus fresh seafood dishes. Finding it is the trick, hidden, as it is, in a residential neighborhood. The No Name had its beginnings in 1935, and is still always packed. Upstairs used to be a brothel. (MM31 Bayside)

BAHIA HONDA STATE PARK ✪ Must See!

(Beach & Park, Bahia Honda Key ☎ 305.872.2353) Bahia Honda's beaches are the most beautiful, most pristine beaches in the Keys—and they boast natural sand (not shipped in from the Bahamas). Two beaches, Sandspur and Calusa, offer 2.5 miles of shore, and the park has about 524 acres. There is camping, picnic areas, nature trails, a bike path, fishing, snorkel gear and kayak rentals, a snack shack and grocery store, and a great view of Henry Flagler's original 7-mile bridge built for a train. Park fees are a mere $3.50 per person, but this is a place visitors can easily spend an entire day. Unlike beaches in nearby Key West, Bahia Honda's waters rarely test positive for contamination. (MM37 Oceanside)

LITTLE DUCK KEY BEACH

(Beach, Little Duck Key) This public beach has rest rooms and picnic shelter, plus a nice little swimming area. The water is shallow with patches of seagrass. Dogs are welcome here, making it a great little lunch stop for people traveling with their family or in RVs. (MM39 Oceanside)

THE MIDDLE KEYS

From Marathon Key to Duck Key, this section highlights a few of the attractions of the middle keys, as you make your way north to the mainland.

ISLAND FISH CO.

(Restaurant, Marathon Key, 12648 Overseas Hwy
☎ 305.743.4191) The menu is extensive at this restaurant and tiki bar, ranging from Florida seafood and Mexican specialties to sandwiches, wraps, pastas, and steaks. There is a fish market attached for fresh seafood-to-go. Food is served at picnic

tables indoors or outdoors in a rustic setting. There is also a gift shop and a bait and tackle store. (MM45 Bayside)

7 MILE GRILL

(Restaurant, Marathon Key, 1240 Overseas Hwy ☎ 305.743.4431) This local's favorite has good food, cold beer, and reasonable prices. It is a converted garage that has been decorated with bumper stickers and an astounding beer can collection. Fried grouper, conch chowder, and the like are the fare here. (MM47.5 Bayside)

PORKY'S

(Restaurant, Marathon Key, 1400 Overseas Hwy ☎ 305.289.2065) This indoor / outdoor dining room beside a lagoon features Creole and Cajun cuisine, plus good old American barbeque. Quirky décor, a laid-back atmosphere, entertainment, and fried Key-Lime pie are draws to this popular eatery. (MM47.5 Bayside)

CASTAWAY

(Restaurant, Marathon Key, 1406 Oceanview Ave ☎ 305.743.6247) Dine inside or out on seafood, burgers, ribs, and the like. It is tricky to find: calling for directions is your best bet. Portions are large, prices are low, and friendly, well-fed cats roam the premise keeping diners company. (MM47.8 Oceanside)

MARATHON TURTLE HOSPITAL ✪ Must See!

(Activity, Marathon Key, 2396 Overseas Hwy ☎ 305.743.4552) Founder Rich Moretti, staff, and volunteers are dedicated to the rescue, rehabilitation, and release of injured sea turtles.

90-minute educational tours introduce visitors to the resident sea turtles and allow visitors to learn about the hospital's
treatments for loggerhead, green, hawksbill and Kemp's ridley
turtles. Make reservations in advance. (MM 48.5 Bayside)

BARRACUDA GRILL

**(Restaurant, Marathon Key, 4290 Overseas Hwy
☎ 305.743.3314)** Though it doesn't look like much from the
outside, Barracuda offers excellent fine dining. The menu is
sophisticated and eclectic, as is the wine menu. Locals rave
about the imaginative cuisine and friendly, competent service.
(MM49.5 Bayside)

SOMBRERO BEACH

(Beach, Marathon Key, Sombrero Beach Rd ☎ 305.289.3000)
This spacious, popular public beach has picnic areas and a playground, and is rarely closed to swimming because of contamination. Visitors love the soft sand, well-maintained volleyball
nets, and the fishing pier. However, during certain times of
the year, stinky, dead seagrass wash ashore can be unpleasant.
(MM50 Oceanside)

CRANE POINT MUSEUM ✪ Must See!

(Natural Museum, Marathon Key ☎ 305.743.9100) This interesting and informative little museum of natural history is
located in a gorgeous, 63-acre hardwood forest. Here, visitors
can learn all about the native flora and fauna so rapidly being
displaced by overdevelopment. The Keys' history comes alive
with interesting historical artifacts. This place is very child-
friendly, with marine touch tanks and an interactive pirate ship
in their children's activity center. The property also has nature

trails that lead to Florida Bay, and houses the Marathon Wild Bird Center. (MM50.5 Bayside)

MARATHON WILD BIRD CENTER

(Activity, Marathon Key ☎ 305.743.8382) Wildlife Rehabilitator Kelly Grinter cares for ill and injured seabirds, songbirds, and raptors here. Grinter and her loyal volunteers have a great facility, complete with lab and surgical area, to insure state-of-the-art care for injured wildlife. Visitors can wander the grounds and observe birds unable to return to the wild and birds on the mend in spacious pens. (MM50.5 Bayside)

CURRY HAMMOCK STATE PARK ✪ Must See!

(Beach, Park, Marathon Key ☎ 850.245.2157) This gorgeous 260-acre park offers a mix of tropical hammock, mangrove swamp, plus a coral rock sand beach. There are grills and picnic tables, plus swings and slides for the kids. Fishing for permit and bonefish in the flats is great, and deeper water on the north side of the park is best for serious swimming and snorkeling (water quality here is usually quite good), and there is a 1.5-mile hiking trail. Tent and R.V. camping is allowed from November to June in certain parts of the park. (MM56.2 Oceanside)

DOLPHIN RESEARCH CENTER

(Activity, Grassy Key ☎ 305.289.1121) This non-profit organization seeks to "promote peaceful coexistence, cooperation, and communication between marine mammals, humans, and the environment we share through research and education." Admission is $20 for adults, $14 for kids. Visitors can meet the dolphins and sea lions and watch trainer sessions with the animals. For significantly more money, interested parties can participate in dolphin swims, play trainer-for-a-day, or other interactive programs. (MM59 Bayside)

THE WRECK & GALLEY GRILL

(Restaurant, Grassy Key, 58835 Overseas Hwy ☎ 305.743.8382) This family-friendly eatery has televisions everywhere showing sports and a grassy side yard for kids. Grouper sandwiches, inexpensive seafood plates, and cheap, cold beer are part of the draw. (MM 59)

THE DOLPHIN CONNECTION

(Activity, Duck Key, Hawk's Cay Resort ☎ 888.814.9154) Make reservations in advance to touch, splash, swim, and play with dolphins in a tropical lagoon for 25 minutes after a 20-minute orientation. Cost is $150, and participants must be 4'6" or taller. Or, for just $60, you can meet the dolphins in an interactive, mostly-dry encounter. Other programs for groups are offered as well. (MM 61 Oceanside)

THE UPPER KEYS

This section highlights a few attractions in the northernmost of the Florida Keys, between Long Key and the mainland.

LONG KEY STATE PARK ✪ Must See!

(Beach & Park, Long Key ☎ 305.664.4815) This 965-acre park has nature trails, campsites, picnic areas, fishing, and swimming. Visitors can rent a canoe and follow a trail through a tidal lagoon. The "beach" here is rocky and the water full of seagrass, making it better for snorkeling than for swim-

ming. There is a reasonable fee to enter the park. (MM67.5
Oceanside)

ANNE'S BEACH

(Beach, Islamorada) This tiny, shallow beach is named after
local environmentalist Anne Eaton. It has a boardwalk through
.3 miles of mangroves, along which hide secluded patches of
beach. There are picnic pavilions and limited parking in two
separate lots. Water quality here is usually fine for swimming.
(MM73.5 Oceanside)

LIGNUMVITAE STATE BOTANICAL PARK

(Activity, Lignumvitae Key ☎ 305.664.2540) Lignumvitae Key
supports a magnificent virgin hardwood hammock, as well as
the 1919 home of the Matheson family, which now serves as
a visitor's center. The park is accessible by boat or kayak only
(leaving Robbie's Marina), and you may not enter the hammock
unless accompanied by a park ranger. Ranger-guided tours are
given twice daily (for a fee). (MM77.5 Bayside)

THE HUNGRY TARPON ✪ Must See!

(Restaurant, Islamorada, 77552 Overseas Hwy ☎ 305.664.0535)
Located at Robbie's Marina, the Hungry Tarpon is open for
breakfast and lunch only. The 60-year-old Conch House maintains its historic vibe. The menu has Keys classics like "Grunts
and Grits", whole fried hogfish, and Cuban black beans. Dine
indoors for air conditioning, or outside to watch visitors feed
the tarpon. (MM77.5 Bayside)

Indian Key State Historical Site

(Nature Park) (Indian Key ☐ 305.664.2540) Accessible only by boat or kayak (available at Robbie's Marina) this 10-acre, uninhabited island has yielded archaeological evidence of prehistoric Native Americans. It housed a thriving settlement in the 1800's, which was destroyed in an attack by Seminoles. Ranger guided tours are available, and there are walking trails and an observation tower. (MM77.5 Oceanside)

LAZY DAYS

(Restaurant, Islamorada ☎ 305.664.5256) This waterfront eatery offers fresh seafood, pasta, steak, etc. on a comfy, shady patio. There's a long, busy bar. They welcome families and large groups, and will gladly cook your catch. (MM79.9 Oceanside)

UNCLES'

(Restaurant, Islamorada, 80939 Overseas Hwy ☎ 305.664.4402) Classic Italian food and lots of it is on the menu. Dine instead or out on the lush patio. The building's outdated, dingy exterior belies the friendly service, extensive wine list, and lush patio you will find inside. They also offer a kiddie menu, vegetarian menu, and heart-smart menu.

LIBRARY BEACH

(Beach, Islamorada) Hidden behind the Islamorada Library is a small, shallow, sandy beach with a playground for the kids. The current can be deceptively strong here, so beware of letting little ones swim unsupervised. Generally, this beach belongs to the locals. (MM81.5 Bayside)

ISLAMORADA FISH CO.

(Restaurant, Islamorada, 81532 Overseas Hwy ☎ 305.664.5690)
This sprawling complex has a restaurant, lounge, and fish
market. There are two bars with dining inside or out. Stone
crab claws, spiny lobster, shrimp, and the like are served in a
casual atmosphere. Portions are generous and the view is fine.
(MM81.5 Bayside)

CHANTICLEER SOUTH

(Restaurant, Islamorada ☎ 305.664.0640) Nantucket chef and
restaurateur Jean-Berruet relocated his French hate cuisine
here in 2005. Reservations are a must—the restaurant has only
11 tables. Foie gras with fruit compote, coq au vin, artisanal
cheeses and the like are paired with excellent French and
Californian wines. Prices are high. (MM81.5 Oceanside)

PIERRE'S ✪ Must See!

(Restaurant, Islamorada ☎ 305.664.3225) Dine indoors
or outdoors for a spectacular view. Haute cuisine with a
Caribbean flair is served with great wine in an elegant, colonial
setting. Prices are steep, but Zagat's, Gourmet, Wine Spectator,
and hundreds of locals have given their accolades to both the
food and service here. (MM81.8 Bayside)

MORADA BAY BEACH CAFÉ & BAR ✪ Must See!

**(Beach & Restaurant, Islamorada, 81950 Overseas Hwy
☎ 305.664.0604)** Dine on a white sand beach at this bayside
bistro, featuring an eclectic menu and superior wine list. The
atmosphere is casually classy without any pretension. Live
entertainment caps off the experience. Prices are mid-range—

less than you'd expect for the romantic location and well-prepared food. (MM81.8 Bayside)

KAIYO ⭐ Must See!

(Restaurant, Islamorada, Old Highway ☎ 305.664.5556) Japan meets Key West in this stylish tea-and-sushi bar. They have a great wine list to pair with dishes like tempura-fried striped bass, Key Lime lobster roll, and noodle bowl with whitewater clams. "Foodies" declare this one of the best restaurants in the Keys. (MM82)

LORELEI

(Restaurant, Islamorada, 96 Madiera Rd ☎ 305.852.4656) This is the other restaurant of the owners of New York City's famous **Tavern on the Green.** It's a casual fish-shack located on a marina, where sunset viewing is optimal. Tables are first-come first-serve (no host/hostess). There is often live music, which can get rather loud. (MM82 Bayside)

BENTLEY'S

(Restaurant, Islamorada, 82779 Overseas Hwy ☎ 305.664.9094) Steak, ribs, and shrimp are served in generous portions at this eclectic, casual-fine-dining bar and grill. The staff is fun and friendly, and the dining room is always packed with locals. (MM82 Oceanside)

ZIGGY & MAD DOG'S

(Restaurant, Islamorada ☎ 305.664.3391) This upscale steakhouse with a beer and wine bar used to be a pineapple plantation. The owners are football stars Howie Long and Terry

Bradshaw. Steaks, pasta, and seafood dishes are on the menu, and prices are high-end. (MM83 Bayside)

BRAZA LENA
(Restaurant, Islamorada, 83413 Overseas Hwy ☎ 305.664.4959) This authentic churrascaria (Brazilian steakhouse) lives at Whale Harbor Marina and does meat like no one else. Traditionally dressed gauchos (meat-carvers) circulate around the abstract-art-decorated dining room. They also have a 50-item salad-and-side-order bar filled with upscale ingredients. (MM83.5 Oceanside)

HOLIDAY ISLE RESORT & MARINA
(Resort, Islamorada ☎ 305.664.2321) You don't have to be a guest to enjoy Holiday Isle's two beaches with water sports concessions, volleyball, tiki bars and waterfront grills—they are all open to the public. But if you do decide to stay a night or two, you can choose between single hotel rooms, self-sufficient "efficiencies", oceanfront suites, or a number of options in between. The resort's entertainment areas are often packed with young, sexy singles partying. The area feels more South Beach, Miami than Florida Keys. (MM84 Oceanside)

THEATER OF THE SEA ✪ Must See!
(Activity, Islamorada, 84721 Overseas Hwy ☎ 305.664.2431) At this educational and entertaining marine animal park, creatures residing in the park's saltwater lagoons and lush gardens include Atlantic bottlenose dolphins, California sea lions, sea turtles, and more. Interactive programs are offered ranging from swimming with dolphins (or sea lions or rays) for good swimmers, to "wading" with dolphins for small children or

those less comfortable in the water. You must reserve well in advance to participate in one of these programs. General Admission ($24 adults, $16 for kids under 12) includes dolphin, sea lion, and parrot shows, a guided tour of marine life exhibits, admission to lagoon-side beach, and the bottomless boat ride. When visiting, don't expect a SeaWorld-type experience; this park is older, smaller and less flashy, and shows are more laid back. (MM84.7 Oceanside)

WINDLEY KEY FOSSIL REEF PARK
(Nature Park, Windley Key, 84900 Overseas Hwy
☎ 305.664.2540) Five short, self-guided trails through a hardwood forest lead to quarries dug out of the limestone, used to build Henry Flagler's railroad. The quarry walls reveal ancient fossilized coral and marine organisms, evidence that 125,000 years ago, the island was under water. There are picnic tables and a visitor center where guests can learn about the local environment. There is a minimal fee to enter the park, and ranger-guided tours are available for slightly more. (MM85.5 Bayside)

CHILLIE WILLIE'S
(Restaurant, Islamorada, 86701 Overseas Hwy ☎ 305.852.8786)
This bar & grill has a game room with plenty of video games, pool table, air hockey, and darts. There are over a dozen televisions playing sporting events. Cheap beer, happy hour, and good bar food keep the locals coming. Kids are welcome here, and good luck getting them out of the game room long enough to eat. (MM86.7 Oceanside)

VILLAGE OF ISLANDS FOUNDERS PARK

(Beach & Park, Islamorada, Plantation Yacht Harbor
☎ 305.852-2381, x502) The bayside beach and water sports concession are open to the public, but the pool is for locals only. Visitors can rent kayaks, clear-bottomed boats, and paddleboats, or just swim, sun and snorkel. There are restrooms on premise, as well as a jogging trail and playgrounds. There is a fee to enter the park. (MM87 Bayside)

MILE MARKER 88

(Restaurant, Islamorada, 88000 Overseas Hwy ☎ 305.852.9315)
This fine dining establishment overlooks Florida Bay. The menu features seafood, steak, and pasta with a "Floribbean" edge. Dine indoors or out. The waitstaff is attractive, if not always attentive. (MM88 Bayside)

THE OLD TAVERNIER

(Restaurant, Tavernier, 90311 Overseas Hwy ☎ 305.852.6012)
Upscale Italian and Greek is served oceanside at this bistro which has been open for over 20 years. The owners, staff, and patrons all have a reputation for being a little eccentric—but that's part of the place's charm. (MM91.8 Oceanside)

HARRY HARRIS PARK

(Park & Beach, Tavernier, Burton Dr ☎ 305.852.7161) This is a great beach for kids, shallow and still. This small beach features a tidal pool protected by a stone jetty. There is a playground, ball field, volleyball, skate park, and picnic grounds. Non-residents must pay a $5 fee on weekends and federal holidays. The water quality almost always tests fine for swimming. (MM92.5 Oceanside)

FLORIDA KEYS WILD BIRD CENTER ✪ Must See!

(Activity, Tavernier, 93600 Overseas Hwy ☎ 305.852.4486)

The FKWBC has a mission: to reduce the suffering of ill and injured wildlife, and to reduce the incidences of their injury through education. There is no admission charge to come and see the birds who can't be released back to the wild, and learn ways you can help prevent injuries to Florida's magnificent wild birds. (MM93.6 Bayside)

BALLYHOO'S

(Restaurant, Key Largo, 9800 Overseas Hwy ☎ 305.852.0822)

Ballyhoo's serves fresh seafood, steaks, and sandwiches in a Conch house from the 1930's made out of County Pine. Beer, shrimp, and wings are paired served alongside more artistic dishes, like Bimini Stuffed Mahi and Yellowfin Tuna Amandine. (MM97.8, on the median)

BIG FISH GRILL

(Restaurant, Key Largo, 99010 Overseas Hwy ☎ 305.451.3734)

Steaks and seafood are served in this slightly upscale sports bar. They also offer live bands, pool table, shuffleboard, and televisions tuned to the game. This place has a friendly, Cheers-like vibe. (MM99 Bayside)

BAYSIDE GRILLE

(Restaurant, Key Largo, 99360 Overseas Hwy ☎ 305.451.3380)

This upscale steak-and-seafood spot has floor-to-ceiling sliding glass door for a fantastic view of sunset over the bay. The fare is American with touches of Italian and Caribbean. Locals and tourists mix freely here. (MM99.5 Bayside)

SNOOK'S ⭐ Must See!

(Restaurant, Key Largo ☎ 305.453.3799) Snook's offers dancing, a Thursday night magic show, a view of the Gulf of Mexico, plus an award winning menu, tapas, brunch, and extensive wine list. The romantic setting and décor make Snook's a frequent setting for weddings. If you can't afford the food, head to the outdoor tiki bar during happy hour for a tropical drink and a gorgeous view. (MM99.9 Bayside)

DOLPHINS PLUS

(Activity, Key Largo, Ocean Bay Dr ☎ 305.451.1993) Swim with dolphins in the facility dedicated to the conservation of marine mammals through education and research. The Atlantic bottlenose porpoises and California Sea lions live in a natural seawater canal. A few different dolphin or sea lion swim programs are offered, as are educational visits. Prices vary greatly according to season, so swimming with these awesome creatures can cost anywhere between $150 and $250 (or higher). Generally, the programs here are designed for capable swimmers. (MM100 Oceanside)

DOLPHIN COVE

(Activity, Key Largo ☎ 305.451.4060) This marine mammal education and dolphin swim center lives on a 5-acre lagoon. They offer structured or unstructured swims with dolphins, priced according to encounter and season, generally between $125 to $245. There is a junior program for kids costing $70. They also offer guided ecological tours of the Everglades back-country and Florida Bay. (MM101.9 Bayside)

JOHN PENNEKAMP CORAL REEF STATE PARK ⊗ Must See!

(Beach & Park, Key Largo ☎ 305.451.1202) Offshore, the
protected coral reef, shipwrecks, and famous "Christ of the
Deep" underwater statue offers the best dive spots in the Keys.
On land, there are three beaches (Canon Beach has remnants
of a Spanish shipwreck 100 feet offshore), a nature trail,
campgrounds, picnic sites, water sports concessions, and more.
There is per-person fee of $3.50 ($1.50 if by foot or bike) to
enter the park. (MM102.5 Oceanside)

CAPTAIN SHON'S

(Restaurant, Key Largo, 103360 Overseas Hwy ☎ 305.453.4000)
This high-end seafood spot features Dungess crab salad,
English-style Fish & Chips and the like in an open-air dining
room. Generally, locals declare this one overpriced tourist trap,
and suggest dining elsewhere. (MM103 Bayside)

EVERGLADES NATIONAL PARK ⊗ Must See!

(Nature Park, Florida City, FL Highway 9336 ☎ 305.242.7700)
The Everglades is made up of several different ecosystems
coexisting within 1.5 million acres, including pinelands, hardwood hammocks, mangroves, and sawgrass prairies. It is
permanent home to countless species of wildlife, and many
migrating species depend on the Everglades for mating and
nesting.

Unfortunately, the Everglades are in trouble. Mankind's
manipulation of natural waterways, pollution of the air and
water, and introduced exotic species of plant and animal are all
chipping away at the once-mighty "Sea of Grass." The govern-

ment has recently approved the Everglades Restoration Plan—the largest environmental restoration project in history.

There is no "mosquito control" in the 'Glades. The best time to visit is the dry season—mid December through mid-April, when there are fewer mosquitoes. Within the park, there are 156 miles of hiking and canoeing trails, several of which are handicap accessible. There are also bike trails, campgrounds, and fishing. Your best bet is to stop off at the one of the visitor centers for maps and info. Visitor Centers and entrances to the park are in different locations, offering a different experience. In Flamingo and Homestead, visitors gain access to a 38-mile road through saw grass prairie, hardwood hammock, cypress swamps, lake regions and Florida Bay. This road offers access to numerous short and long trails. Shark Valley has the entrance to the Tamiami Trail through the saw grass prairie. Everglades City is the jumping-off spot to the Ten Thousand Islands, a mangrove estuary great for anglers.

Entrance fees to the park are $10 per vehicle (more if you're towing a boat), and are good for 7 days. There is no longer a hotel and restaurant within the park itself (Flamingo Hotel was destroyed by Hurricane Wilma) but lodging and dining is abundant in the surrounding towns. **Flamingo Marina** *(☎ 239.695.3101)* has a convenience store, dockage, boat and car fuel, dockage, eco-tours, and fishing charters. While within the Everglades National Park, please be careful and follow park rules. This is for your own safety, as well as the safety of this fragile ecosystem and the wildlife within.

Quick Reference Top 5's

In this section for easy reference you will find "Top 5's." Whether you are traveling with children or on your honeymoon, interested in birdwatching or partying, you will be able to find at least five places in Key West that appeals to you.

FOR KIDS
1. Key West Aquarium
2. Glassbottom Boat Discovery
3. Key West Toy Factory
4. Smather's Beach
5. Best Western Hibiscus Hotel

FOR HONEYMOONERS
1. Danger charter's "Wind and Wine" Sunset Cruise
2. Lattitudes restaurant
3. Duval House hotel
4. Louie's Backyard "afterdeck" bar
5. Fort Zachary Taylor beach

FOR SPRING BREAKERS
1. Rick's nightclub
2. Smather's beach
3. Fat Tuesday bar
4. Pegasus Hotel
5. Caroline's restaurant

GAY GETAWAYS
1. 801 Bourbon St. Pub
2. Big Ruby's Guesthouse
3. Skinny Dipper sunset tour
4. Square One restaurant
5. LaTeDa cabaret

LESBIAN GETAWAYS
1. Pearl's Rainbow guesthouse
2. Venus fishing, snorkeling, or dolphin watching excursion
3. Pearl's Patio bar
4. Aqua nightclub
5. Fairvilla Megastore

FOR BIRDWATCHERS
1. Dry Tortugas Nat'l Park
2. Ft. Zachary Taylor State Park
3. Key West Wildlife Ctr
4. Little Hamaca Park
5. Key West Tropical Forest and Botanical Gardens

FOR HORTICULTURISTS

1. Key West Tropical Forest and Botanical Gardens
2. West Martello Museum (Key West Garden Club)
3. Nancy Forester's Secret Garden
4. Key West Butterfly and Nature Conservatory
5. Sonny McCoy Indigenous Park

FOR ECO-TOURISTS

1. Dry Tortugas National Park
2. Key West Extreme Adventures Shark Tour
3. Sunny Day's "Island Express" to Looe Key
4. Sonny McCoy Indigenous Park / Key West Wildlife Center
5. Key Deer Refuge (Big Pine Key)

FOR ART COLLECTORS

1. Luis Sottiel Gallery
2. Thomas Kinkade Gallery
3. Key West Gallery
4. Gingerbread Square Gallery
5. Kent Gallery

FOR HISTORY BUFFS

1. Fort Zachary Taylor
2. Harry S. Truman Little White House
3. USS Mohawk CGC Memorial Museum
4. Mel Fisher's Maritime Museum
5. Artist House hotel

FOR LITERATI

1. Key West Literary Seminar
2. Hemingway Home
3. Crown Plaza de la Concha
4. Authors Guesthouse
5. Captain Tony's Saloon

FINE DINING

1. Ambrosia (Japanese)
2. Antonia's (Italian)
3. Square One (American)
4. Lattitudes (American)
5. Pisces (French)

CASUAL DINING

1. Maison de Pepe (Cuban)
2. Banana Cafe (French)
3. Thai Life Floating Cafe (Thai)
4. Salsa Loca (Mexican)
5. Seven Fish (American)

BEACHES IN THE FLORIDA KEYS

1. Fort Jefferson beach (Dry Tortugas National Park)
2. Sandspur Beach (Bahia Honda State Park)
3. Fort Zachary Taylor beach (Key West)
4. Sombrero Beach (Marathon) Calusa Beach (Bahia Honda State Park)
5. Smather's beach (Key West)

HAPPY HOURS

1. Conch Republic Seafood Company
2. Alonzo's Oyster Bar
3. Southernmost Beach Cafe
4. Kelly's
5. Schooner Wharf

PLACES TO DANCE 'TILL DAWN

1. Virgilio's
2. Rick's
3. Upstairs at Mangos
4. Martin's (Saturdays)
5. El Maison de Pepe (weekends)

THINGS TO DO FOR FREE

1. Smather's Beach
2. Key West Wildlife Center
3. Dog Beach
4. Little Hamaca Park
5. Sheriff's Zoo

"LOCALS" HANGOUTS

1. The Porch wine bar
2. Bottlecap bar
3. Tropic Cinema
4. Bobby's Monkey Bar
5. Studios of Key West

PLACES ONLY TOURISTS GO

1. Southernmost Point
2. Sloppy Joe's bar
3. Margaritaville
4. Higgs Beach
5. Hard Rock Cafe

Top 5

Index

Index

About the Author

Sarah Goodwin-Nguyen and husband Andrew moved to Key West from New York City in 2005. Since then, she has worked as a freelance writer, wildlife rehabilitator, aquarist, tour guide, and restaurateur. Besides travel writing, she writes poetry, fiction, book reviews, and web content. Her monthly column, "Key West Confidential," appears in *Key West History* magazine.

Astoria

Astoria, Oregon was the West Coast's first permanent American settlement. The city and surrounding areas have been the location of choice for many Hollywood blockbusters as well as for vacationers looking to see the state's beautiful North Coast.

Price: $14.95; ISBN: 978-1-935455-08-0

Biloxi

Explore Biloxi and the Mississippi Gulf Coast. Find the best place to get a bowl of seafood gumbo and the most enjoyable golf course. From casinos to beaches, Biloxi and Gulfport offer great vacation opportunities.

Price: $14.95; ISBN: 978-1-935455-09-7

Black Hills (2nd Edition)

Revised and updated, use this guide to discover the striking natural beauty, abundant wildlife, and many attractions that the Black Hills has to offer, from the iconic Mount Rushmore to the historic Mammoth Site.

Price: $14.95; ISBN: 978-1-935455-10-3

Branson

Explore Branson, Missouri and the Ozarks. This completely independent guide will help you plan the perfect vacation, with information about the best shows in town and other attractions in the Lakes Area. Learn why many call Branson "America's favorite hometown."

Price: $14.95; ISBN: 978-1-935455-11-0

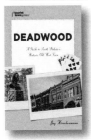

Deadwood

This independent book will help you plan the perfect vacation to the historic town of Deadwood, in the heart of South Dakota's Black Hills. Stroll the streets where Wild Bill Hickok and Calamity Jane once lived.

Price: $13.95; ISBN: 978-1-935455-22-6

Door County

This independent guide will help you plan the perfect vacation to Wisconsin's thumb, including must-see attractions and the best outdoor activities. Hit the streets shopping, sit down for dinner overlooking the water, and discover the hidden natural beauty of Door County.

Price: $14.95; ISBN: 978-1-935455-12-7

Fredericksburg

Explore Fredericksburg's must-see attractions, find the best places for wine enthusiasts, and learn about the area's German heritage with this independent guide. Get the most out of your next visit to the Texas Hill Country.

Price: $14.95; ISBN: 978-1-935455-13-4

Key West (3rd Edition)

There is much to see and do in Key West, a vacation hotspot welcoming millions of visitors each year. In this guide, learn about area beaches, restaurants and bars, Duval Street attractions, hotels, and more. This book will help you plan your next vacation to the Conch Republic.

Price: $14.95; ISBN: 978-1-935455-14-1

Lake Placid

Look down a ski jump, hike the high peaks, and learn to dogsled. Explore the picturesque Village of Lake Placid, New York, and the surrounding Adirondacks. Also discover the best of nearby Lake George and Saranac Lake.

Price: $14.95; ISBN: 978-1-935455-15-8

Mackinac (2nd Edition)

Nestled between Michigan's Upper and Lower Peninsulas, Mackinac Island is a favorite tourist destination and a beautiful getaway spot. This guide will help you plan your vacation to Mackinac Island and Mackinaw City.

Price: $14.95; ISBN: 978-1-935455-16-5

Madison County

Explore the picturesque landscape and historic covered bridges of Madison County, Iowa. Whether planning to photograph the bridges, sample the local wine, or take take a step back in time, make your journey a memorable one.

Price: $13.95; ISBN: 978-1-935455-17-2

Mystic

This guide to the historic Connecticut seaport city of Mystic will help you plan the perfect vacation, with comprehensive information about the Mystic Seaport, the best places to shop, dine and sleep, and must-see attractions.

Price: $14.95; ISBN: 978-1-935455-18-9

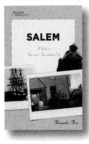

Salem

This independent guidebook will help you plan the perfect vacation to Massachusetts' historic seaport and site of the Salem Witch Trials, with information about the best historic attractions, Halloween and Haunted Happenings, and more.

Price: $14.95; ISBN: 978-1-935455-19-6

Sleepy Hollow

Washington Irving immortalized Sleepy Hollow and Tarrytown in his classic tale. This independent guide will help you plan the perfect vacation, with comprehensive information about must-see Historic Hudson Valley estates, facts and fictions of Sleepy Hollow, and more.

Price: $13.95; ISBN: 978-1-935455-20-2

Solvang

Plan the perfect vacation to America's Danish Capital. Learn about must-see area landmarks and highlights of the Santa Ynez Valley. From aebleskiver to vineyards and windmills, use this guide to travel prepared.

Price: $13.95; ISBN: 978-1-935455-21-9

tourist town guides

www.touristtown.com

Also Available

TITLE	ISBN	PRICE
Atlantic City	978-1-935455-00-2	$14.95
Breckenridge	978-0-9767064-9-6	$14.95
Frankenmuth	978-0-9767064-8-9	$13.95
Gatlinburg	978-1-935455-04-2	$14.95
Hershey	978-0-9792043-8-8	$13.95
Hilton Head	978-1-935455-06-6	$14.95
Jackson Hole	978-0-9792043-3-3	$14.95
Las Vegas	978-0-9792043-5-7	$14.95
Myrtle Beach	978-1-935455-01-1	$14.95
Niagara Falls	978-1-935455-03-5	$14.95
Ocean City	978-0-9767064-6-5	$13.95
Provincetown	978-1-935455-07-3	$13.95
Sandusky	978-0-9767064-5-8	$13.95
Williamsburg	978-1-935455-05-9	$14.95
Wisconsin Dells	978-0-9792043-9-5	$13.95

See http://www.touristtown.com for more information about any of these titles.

www.touristtown.com

ORDER FORM
ON REVERSE SIDE

Tourist Town Guides® is published by:
Channel Lake, Inc.
P.O. Box 1771
New York, NY 10156

tourist town guides®

ORDER FORM

Telephone: With your credit card handy, call toll-free 800.592.1566

Fax: Send this form toll-free to 866.794.5507

E-mail: Send the information on this form to orders@channellake.com

Postal mail: Send this form with payment to Channel Lake, Inc. P.O. Box 1771, New York, NY, 10156

Your Information: ( ) Do not add me to your mailing list

Name: _____

Address: _____

City: _____ State: _____ Zip: _____

Telephone: _____

E-mail: _____

Book Title(s) / ISBN(s) / Quantity / Price
(see www.touristtown.com for this information)

_____

_____

_____

Total payment*: $_____

Payment Information: (Circle One) Visa / Mastercard

Number: _____ Exp: _____

Or, make check payable to: **Channel Lake, Inc.**

* Add the lesser of $6.50 USD or 18% of the total purchase price for shipping. International orders call or e-mail first! New York orders add 8% sales tax.